In His Mercy
Understanding the Thirteen Midot

Ezra Bick

IN HIS MERCY

UNDERSTANDING THE THIRTEEN MIDOT

TRANSLATED BY

David Silverberg

Yeshivat Har Etzion
Maggid Books

In His Mercy
Understanding the Thirteen Midot

First English Edition, 2011

Maggid Books
An imprint of Koren Publishers Jerusalem Ltd.

POB 8531, New Milford, CT 06776-8531, USA
& POB 4044, Jerusalem 91040, Israel

www.korenpub.com

Originally published as
Yud-Gimmel Midot Shel Raḥamim [Hebrew]

ISBN 978-1-59264-757-6, *paperback*

A CIP catalogue record for this title is
available from the British Library

Printed and bound in USA

לעילוי נשמת יהושע בן הלל ע״ה

Dedicated in loving memory of

Richard J. Silvera ע״ה

by his children
Hillel, Albert and Michelle

Contents

Preface

This book is based on a series of lectures delivered in Hebrew at Yeshivat Har Etzion during the month of Elul over the course of some twenty years, which were subsequently transcribed to form the basis for a course in the Israel Koschitzky Virtual Beit Midrash of Yeshivat Har Etzion. A Hebrew book based on these lectures was published in the summer of 2009. This English edition was elegantly translated by Rabbi David Silverberg.

Over the years, the ideas in these lectures were developed in discussions with my students, too many to be enumerated here. The chief objective of these discussions was to understand *why* we recite the Thirteen Attributes of Mercy in the *Seliḥot* prayer; the secondary goal was to understand each attribute based on the Talmud, midrashim, and major commentaries. This method was successful with most of the attributes, and I had only to expand somewhat on the statements of the sages. Despite this, a great deal of effort was invested in understanding the deep philosophical underpinnings of those statements, and I therefore pray that this book will contribute to readers' understanding.

Many of the basic principles regarding the nature of man, sin, the relationship between the sinner and God, and the creation of the world involve subtle distinctions that flowed naturally in oral presentation and discussion, but which may be less clear in writing. When my students presented their plan to publish these lectures in written form, I was concerned – and still am – that the direct personal interchange present in the original format was a necessary ingredient in understanding the ideas. Nevertheless, I agreed to their plan, editing as well as adding to the original work.

My hope is that by broadening the audience for these discussions, the ideas will be further elucidated. I therefore request that any reader who has a question, an idea to add, a point to clarify, or any comment communicate with me so that the process begun more than twenty years ago can continue. This book is a classic illustration of "from my disciples more than from any other," and I am certain that only through continued group discussion of scholars, students, and anyone concerned with the service of God will we advance towards greater understanding of these topics.

My sincere hope is that, aside from contributing philosophical understanding, these lectures will add to the experience of prayer and petition of the Jewish people, to the revelation in this world of the grace and mercy of the King of Mercy, and to the redemption of the world and the Kingdom of Israel.

Ezra Bick
Erev Rosh Ḥodesh Adar Bet 5771
Alon Shvut

Introduction

There is a widespread custom to recite the *Seliḥot* service on fast days, during the month of Elul, and on Yom Kippur. The service revolves around the recitation of the Thirteen *Midot HaRaḥamim* (Attributes of Mercy), which were revealed to Moses *BeNikrat HaTzur,* in the cleft of the rock, when he ascended Har Sinai to receive the second set of *luḥot* (tablets):

> HaShem descended in a cloud and stood with him there, and he called out with the name of HaShem. HaShem passed before him and proclaimed: "*HaShem, HaShem, El Raḥum veḤanun, Erekh Apayim, veRav Ḥesed veEmet, Notzer Ḥesed laAlafim, Noseh Avon vaFesha veḤata'a veNakeh* – but does not cleanse completely, recalling the iniquity of parents upon children and grandchildren to the third and fourth generations"... He said, "Behold, I seal a covenant: Before your entire people I shall perform wonders such as have never been created in the entire world and among all the nations..." (Exodus 35:4–10)

While there is no explicit Talmudic source for the custom to recite *Seliḥot,* the Gemara addresses the general concept of reciting the Thirteen Attributes. In the context of a discussion about the annual judgment on the Days of Awe and the great Day of Judgment at the end of days, the Gemara expounds on God's revelation of the Thirteen Attributes to Moses:

> "The Lord passed in front of him and called..." [Exodus 34:6]: R. Yoḥanan said: Had the verse not been written, it would have been impossible to say it – this teaches that the Almighty wrapped Himself as a *shali'aḥ tzibbur* [leader of the public prayer service] and showed Moses the prayer service. He said to him, "Any time Israel sins, let them perform this service before Me and I shall forgive them." (*Rosh HaShana* 17b)

Later in the same Talmudic passage, we read:

> R. Yehuda said: A covenant has been made with the Thirteen Attributes that they do not return empty-handed [without achieving their desired goal], as it says, "Behold, I make a covenant" [Exodus 34:10].

According to R. Yehuda, the "covenant" that God announces after the revelation of the Thirteen Attributes pertains to the attributes themselves. The significance of the Attributes' status as a "covenant" lies in the commitment that the One who initiated the covenant – the Almighty – made to the *Benei Yisrael* (*Children of Israel*). After presenting the Thirteen Attributes, God said to Moses, "Behold, I make a covenant: I shall perform wonders in view of your entire nation..." Normal prayer does not guarantee a response; some prayers indeed return "empty-handed." But a prayer involving a covenant implies mutual responsibility and a commitment between the Almighty and the *Benei Yisrael,* and hence demands a response – even if that response must take the form of "wonders." God's covenant ensures that the prayer of the Thirteen Attributes will always be effective.

Thus, during times of supplication and intense prayer, such as the *Yamim Nora'im* (the Days of Awe), we recite *Seliḥot* as part of the process of repentance. At a time when we plead for mercy, we perform the service that God assured Moses will always be effective – the recitation of the Thirteen Attributes.

This enigmatic passage raises a number of questions, however. R. Yoḥanan comments that there is something about the Torah's description of this event that is so unimaginable that were it not for the special permission granted by the Scriptural account, we would not be able to articulate it ourselves – "Had the verse not been written, it would have been impossible to say it." What is so astonishing about God's revelation here?

Furthermore, according to R. Yoḥanan, "God wrapped Himself as a *shali'aḥ tzibbur* and showed Moses the prayer service" – God revealed the Thirteen Attributes, which are essentially a prayer, by presenting Himself as a *ḥazan* leading the congregation in their recitation. The opening line of the narrative – "HaShem passed in front of him and called" – is not an introduction of what God said to Moses, but rather a visual demonstration of what the Jewish People should do when they pray. But in what sense does a list of God's attributes constitute prayer or supplication? After all, we have nothing here but a list of names and descriptions of God! This is certainly not a prayer in the normal sense, as it entails no request or petition. How can such a "prayer service" bring about atonement, let alone guarantee it?

Indeed, the Thirteen *Midot HaRaḥamim* themselves are not so novel as to be unmentionable. The astounding idea revealed in this narrative relates to the Thirteen Attributes as a prayer service recited before the Almighty. Had God Himself not demonstrated the possibility that the Thirteen Attributes serve as a medium of prayer through which we achieve atonement, we would have been unable to imagine it on our own. But what, indeed, is the secret to the power of this unusual "prayer"? And if a simple recitation of the Attributes is effective, why was a special demonstration necessary to teach Moses how to perform the service properly?

A CHARIOT FOR THE *SHEKHINA*

I believe that the fundamental basis of *Seliḥot* is found in a basic concept of Jewish thought that lies at the heart of our relationship with the Almighty – God's presence in this world depends on human initiative. The revelation of the Divine Glory is carried upon a human "chariot." In other words, the *Shekhina* resides in the space that human beings make for it. In the context of prayer, this means that the Almighty is revealed to the same degree to which people call out to Him.

The interplay between God's presence and human action is illustrated through the concept of God's *Malkhut*, His Kingship. An ancient saying declares that *"ein melekh belo am"* – "there is no king without a people." When subjects proclaim, "Long live the king!" they do not simply express their acknowledgment to the king that he is king, as though declaring to a wall that it is a wall. "Long live the king" is a declaration of loyalty that yields two related results – the nation accepts the yoke of kingship and, correspondingly, the king's royal status is enhanced. Thus, the declaration *effects* kingship, and does not merely *attest* to it; the pronouncement is not merely descriptive, but constitutive. The nation's declaration of loyalty *creates* the king's kingship, for if the nation does not acknowledge his kingship, by definition he is not a king.

This is true of mortal kings, and it is true of the King of the universe as well. When we declare, *"HaShem Melekh, HaShem Malakh, HaShem Yimlokh LeOlam VaEd"* ("The Lord reigns, the Lord has reigned, that Lord shall reign for all eternity!"), we not only acknowledge the past and present, but also commit ourselves to accepting divine kingship, and thereby crown God for all eternity. Our acceptance of divine kingship is thus significant not only for us, but for the kingship itself, for it is our acceptance that establishes it.

R. Baḥya (Genesis 38:30) cites the principle of *"ein melekh belo am"* to explain why we celebrate the kingship of God on Rosh HaShana – it is only after creation that God is truly King, for there is no king without a nation.[1] The source for this idea is apparently a midrash in *Pirkei DeRabbi Eliezer* (ch. 3):

1. The accepted opinion is that Rosh HaShana marks the day of the creation of Man.

> God immediately consulted the Torah, whose name is Strength, to create the world. She answered Him and said: Master of the Universe, if the King has no army and He has no camp, over what shall He rule? And if there is no people to praise the King, what honor of the King is there?

Rosh HaShana not only commemorates the Almighty's kingship as an annual celebration of the historical day of His ascension on the throne, but rather constitutes the actual coronation repeated each and every year. On Rosh HaShana, we place a crown on God's head, so to speak. As we say in the High Holiday prayer service, "*Veyitenu Lekha keter melukha*" – "and they shall give You a royal crown."

How can human beings, mere subjects of the King, coronate[2] God? How can a lowly creature crown the Supreme Being? The answer is simple. The concept of kingship is rooted in the subjects' submission of their will to the ruler's will. Through our active acceptance of His rule, we create the kingship of God.

As difficult as this concept is to understand, it is sung by Jewish children throughout the world in their daily prayers when they recite "*Adon Olam*:"

> Master of the World, who reigned before any creature was created;
> At the time when all by His will is done, then His name is called, "King."

On the one hand, God is King even "before any creature was created" – even if no world exists. On the other hand, only when all has been done in accordance with His will can we say that "His name was called 'King.'" The "name" of God refers to how He is known among the world's creatures, and hence depends upon His creatures' acceptance

---

This is expressed in the *Zikhronot* prayer on Rosh HaShana: "This day is the beginning of Your creations, a remembrance of the first day."

2. The common Hebrew verb "*lehamlikh*," found throughout the daily prayers, means to make someone king, and has no simple English equivalent. We use "coronate" to designate this verb.

of His Kingship and their performance of His will. If no one truly calls His name – if no one recognizes His Kingship – this would undermine the concept of God's Kingship, at least to the extent to which the term describes a connection to and presence in the world.[3]

STATIC AND DYNAMIC KINGSHIP

The language of the midrash in *Pirkei DeRabbi Eliezer* implies two aspects of kingship. One, characterized by the terms "army and camp," refers to the power of the King. The army exemplifies the might of the King, His executive power, the force that enables His will to be carried out. In other words, the King is the ruler, whose word is law. In a world where free will is present, God's word is not fulfilled simply as a result of His will, but only by the assent of the will of the governed. Hence, disobedience, non-acceptance of His will, is a negation of His kingship itself. In this aspect of kingship, acceptance of the yoke of Heaven leads directly to the acceptance of the yoke of the commandments.

However, the midrash refers to a second aspect of God's kingship: "If no one praises the King, where is the honor of the King?" This aspect of kingship is alien to the modern democratic mind. The hallmark of kingship is seen not in obedience or fulfillment of the commandments, but in praise of God – "*Kevod Malkhuto*," the honor of the King. God's kingship over the world has an aspect of majesty, of dignity and honor, which is expressed by the relationship of the people to the personality of the King – through *shir vashevaḥ*, song and praise – and not only through their acceptance of His authority. Honoring the majesty of God is very different than merely obeying His commands.[4]

---

3. We read in *Mishlei* (14:28), "In the multitude of people is the honor of the king, but the negation of people is the destruction of the prince." R. Baḥya writes (introduction to Numbers 23): "The absence of the people destroys him, until the name of king is removed and he is no more than one of the princes who rules the people. Therefore, the verse calls him 'prince' and not 'king,' for there is no king without a people." This explanation refers to a mortal king, but the sages famously applied this verse to the King of the World as well.

4. According to the perspective that the kingship of God depends on the world over which He rules, there is a further dimension of kingship in the rule over human beings, who possess free will and freely accept His rule over them. Kingship over the natural world exists from the moment of creation, but kingship in the world

God's honor as King is also referred to as "*Shem HaShem*," since the "name" is articulated through speech. Indeed, the midrash suggests (*Bereshit Raba* 39:16) that this is what it means to "call in the name of God," as Abraham did upon arriving in *Eretz Yisrael* (the Land of Israel) – "He caused the name of God to be called in the mouths of people" by leading them all to honor the name of God.[5] "Calling in the name of God" does not mean speaking to Him, but rather establishing His existence and presence in the world. It is not a means of bringing about the *Shekhina*'s presence, but rather the presence itself.

The midrash offers a second interpretation of this phrase as well. When Abraham "called in the name of God," he "converted them and brought them under the wings of the *Shekhina*" – he convinced others to accept God's will as law.[6] It is impossible to divorce the kingship of speech from the kingship of action, the kingship of prayer from the kingship of mitzva observance.

There is a basic distinction between the two aspects of kingship, however. In the realm of mitzva observance, it is possible to conceive of a static situation. The kingship of God may be said to be intact as long as there is no opposition to the rule of God, even if there is no active observance of the mitzvot, because there is no immediate command

---

of freedom begins only from the giving of the Torah at Sinai. This is not merely a quantitative difference; kingship accepted out of free will is a totally different type of kingship, a higher qualitative aspect of *Malkhut*. The Vilna Gaon explains that this is the difference between *Memshala*, which is expressed through the irresistible power of God, and *Melukha*, which is based on free will and acceptance. In the case of free choice, the kingship is measured not only by the results – so many servants, so many acts of obedience – but in the process and the act by which man freely chooses God as his King. In the midrash from *Pirkei DeRabbi Eliezer*, this qualitative factor was referred to as "the honor of His kingship" and was expressed through the praise that the people offer to the King, as opposed to the army, which is subservient to the King.

5. The Ramban similarly explains: "The correct explanation is that he called out God's name in a great voice, there, before the altar, to announce God's existence and his divinity to humankind… And he was trained to teach and to publicize the nature of God."

6. According to this interpretation, to call God's name similarly implies bringing God's presence into the world, as it means to work towards the goal that His kingship will spread throughout the world.

to obey. However, in the realm of the majesty of God, the kingship of God demands constant honor. In the words of the midrash, the *kilus*, the praise of God, never reaches its limit. The Gemara (*Berakhot* 33b) describes a *ḥazan* who extended a long list of praises for God, many more than in the customary prayer. R. Ḥanina waited until he finished and then berated him, "Have you finished all the praises of our Master?!"

The act of proclaiming God's kingship does not preserve the kingship, but renews it and increases it at every moment. The majesty of God is renewed by the people who acclaim Him. Even if it appears to the outside observer that nothing has changed, the relationship between the people and the King is a dynamic process of creativity, magnification, and perfection.

This sense of constantly renewed kingship is expressed in the phrase, "God ruled, God rules, God shall rule forever and ever." On the one hand, this emphasizes the constancy of God's kingship – *that which was* is *what shall be*, exactly as before, for all eternity. In a static situation, where the present is frozen for eternity, existence is only the present. But when the present can only remain unchanged if it is renewed constantly every instant, it is described in Hebrew through the use of the continual future progressive. The future tense of "shall rule," when conjoined with the limitlessness of "forever and ever," emphasizes that God ascends the throne of His kingship at every individual moment, and the continuation of this process depends on the active proclamation of the people, the subjects of the King who praise Him. This act of continual coronation is also true of the first aspect of kingship, the power of the King; the acceptance of the yoke of heaven proclaims God's kingship anew every second.

MANIFESTATION OF THE ATTRIBUTES

The principle illustrated by God's *Malkhut* – that the revelation of His kingship depends on the people's acceptance of it – underlies all of the divine attributes. The *Shekhina* is revealed in accordance with human awareness. Indeed, the very concept of creation entails that these attributes are manifest in the world through the means of man's actions. Before creation, God lacked nothing – in the absolute sense, He was the King and Judge, compassionate and good, mighty and great – and so will He continue to be when nothing exists at all. Creation signifies the decision of the absolute God to reveal Himself through relative attributes – to be not only the King, but King over a people; to be not only compassionate, but to be a compassionate ruler of the Earth; to be not only God, but to be our God and us His people. Without human recognition, then, a given attribute cannot be manifested in the world.[7]

Although the existence of God's attributes is not dependent on the world's existence, the creation of the world added the *relative* quality of the divine attributes, which resulted in the total dependency of the Divine Presence on the free-willed acceptance of the creatures. If the Almighty were to force Himself upon the world – if He were to reveal Himself without prior invitation – He would negate the entire achievement of the initial act of creation. Indeed, if human beings would not invite God into the world, the world would cease to serve as an arena of divine revelation and a chariot of God.

When the Gemara states that God's covenant with *Benei Yisrael* ensures that the Thirteen Attributes will not "return empty-handed," it does not mean that if we do our part by reciting the list, God will do His by granting forgiveness. Our part of the "bargain" is much deeper than that. Declaring the Thirteen Attributes – recognition of God's names of

---

7. One might argue that not only is the world, and specifically man, the vehicle that enables the kingship of God, but this goal is actually the entire purpose of creation – God created the world in order to achieve the degree of kingship that can only exist when there are people who accept His kingship. According to this argument, the existence of the world *contributes* to the perfection of God by adding another dimension to His kingship. This claim was developed primarily within the world of Hasidism. The Ba'al HaTanya, for example, writes, "Now it is well-known to all that the purpose of creation was to reveal the kingship of God, for there is no king without a nation" (*Sha'ar HaYiḥud*, ch. 7).

   This explanation differs from the position adopted by the Rambam, who argues that it is impossible to offer any explanation for why God created the world, since the world cannot add anything to God's perfection. It also differs from the explanation advanced by R. Hasdai Crescas, who argued that the existence of the world is a result of the principle, "It is the nature of the good to do good" – that the world is a result of God's moral perfection. Accordingly, the external existence of the world is an expression of the inner perfection of God.

compassion – directly results in their manifestation in the world. Indeed, the Almighty appears to the same degree to which man calls His name.

When we read these Attributes of Mercy, the *Shekhina*'s manifestation must, by necessity, take the form of mercy. In fact, the will of the *Shekhina* to reside in the lower world requires that we call out the Attributes of Mercy, for the very presence of these divine names in the mouths of humans constitutes the presence of mercy in the world.

According to what we have said, we are the ones who determine the nature of God's presence in the world. If we do not call out in the name of God, He will not be present! This statement, upon reflection, is truly astounding. Can a human banish the divine King of Kings from his throne? Do we control, as it were, the presence of the King? As R. Yoḥanan tells us, "Had the verse not been written, it would have been impossible to say it!" It would indeed be impossible to say such a thing had God Himself not informed us that this is in fact the case!

In fact, the concept of man's ability to draw the Divine Presence into the world is so implausible that God could not simply relate it verbally to Moses – He had to demonstrate it. Even if man is the chariot of the *Shekhina*, the actual descent of the *Shekhina* onto that chariot must come from God. We can express our readiness to serve as the chariot by proclaiming God's attributes, and we may crown God and thereby establish His kingship. But the remarkable merging of the King of Kings – whom even the highest reaches of the heavens cannot possibly contain – with the lower world, the four cubits of man, is possible only because God bestows His *Shekhina* upon the world.

Until Moses personally witnessed God calling out the Attributes of Mercy, he could not imagine any person doing so. Who stands in front of the congregation, wrapped in a *tallit*, calling out the names of God? Who leads them in bringing down the *Shekhina*? "The Almighty wrapped Himself as a *shali'aḥ tzibbur*..." The human *shali'aḥ tzibbur* who leads the *Seliḥot* does not ask God to appear, but rather substantiates the *Shekhina*.

"Any time Israel sins, let them perform this service before Me..." We are instructed to perform this very service, but not simply by repeating the formula. In a standard prayer service, we stand on one side, *facing* God. During *Seliḥot*, in contrast, we stand not opposite the *Shekhina*, but rather *amidst* the *Shekhina*; we are surrounded by It and bring about

Its manifestation in our midst. God Himself is situated at the head of the congregation forming the chariot; He does not listen to this prayer service, He is present within it. Had the verse not been written, it would have been impossible to say such a thing!

"HaShem descended in a cloud and stood with him there, and he called out with the name of HaShem" – God called in His own name. When we call in His name and establish His presence, He calls His name, and is thus revealed. The mention of God's name in our mouths constitutes the manifestation of the *Shekhina* in the world.

THE STRENGTH OF THE LORD

In light of what we have argued here, we have the power, through the recitation of the Thirteen Attributes, to "strengthen" God. After the sin of the spies, Moses invokes the revelation he experienced in the *nikrat hatzur* to achieve atonement for Israel (Numbers 14:17–18). He introduces his petition for forgiveness by requesting, "*Ve'ata yigdal na ko'aḥ HaShem ka'asher dibarta…*," "And now, may the strength of the Lord be increased, as You spoke…" God is indeed exalted and magnified as a result of the recitation of the Thirteen Attributes; His strength in the world increases and intensifies.

According to the Aristotelian philosophy of the Middle Ages, such a notion is a logical absurdity – an absolute God can never grow or increase. Moses, however, understood the secret revealed to him in the cleft of the rock at Sinai. God's strength and presence in our world indeed increase through people, including sinners – and perhaps specifically through sinners – who turn to Him and call in His name. This increase of God's "strength" is the basis of forgiveness, which itself constitutes the basis of the continued existence of a world that had been sentenced to destruction just a moment earlier, when the "strength" of compassion and its manifestation were weaker, and hence insufficient.

Since kingship depends on its acceptance by the subjects of a king, it follows that the value of kingship is relative and that it can increase or decrease; the more the people accept the authority of a king and the greater the number of people who count themselves as that king's subjects, the greater the kingship itself. The same is true of God's other attributes as well; the more people who recognize God's compassion, the more it is present in the world.

THE ATTRIBUTES AS PRAYER

The Gemara emphasizes that the Attributes serve as a "*seder tefilla*" – an order of prayer. The sages who arranged the *Seliḥot* service made a point of ensuring that it would follow the same structure as the standard Minḥa prayer service. We begin with *Ashrei* and half-Kaddish, followed by verses of praise describing the greatness of God, corresponding to the first three *berakhot* of the *Amida* prayer. We then proceed to the Thirteen Attributes and conclude with *Taḥanun* and *Kaddish Titkabel*. Nevertheless, there is a vast difference between regular prayer and the recitation of the Thirteen Attributes. At the heart of the standard prayer service lie the thirteen blessings of the main body of the *Amida*, in which we present our requests to God. Correspondingly, the *Seliḥot* service revolves around the Thirteen Attributes – but this recitation contains no requests or petitions. How can this be called a "prayer service," an "order of prayer"?

The sages describe prayer as "*avoda shebalev*" – "service of the heart." Why should our requests be termed "service," as if we are slaves serving our master? By turning to God to fill all our needs, we express our recognition of the fact that everything depends on the King; we place God at the center of our lives. Thus, the requests we present in the *Amida* constitute an act of *avodat HaShem*, serving the King, for they declare that we are totally dependent on Him, as a slave is dependent on his master.

In the *Seliḥot*, we serve God in a more direct fashion – we make ourselves a chariot for the *Shekhina* in the world, the basis for His kingship and presence in the world He created. This is *avodat HaShem*, a servant's service to his Master, in the simplest sense of the term. While it is important that we understand the meaning of each of God's Attributes of Mercy, the underlying principle behind reciting them is our readiness to serve as the bearers of the *Shekhina* in the world. Through *Seliḥot*, we enable God to sit on the royal throne of compassion and kindness.[8]

---

8. This is why the *Seliḥot* have the status of a *davar shebikedusha* and therefore require a *minyan*; see Appendix I.

Thus, "a covenant has been made with the Thirteen Attributes that they do not return empty-handed." If the recitation of these Attributes would not achieve their desired goal of bringing God's presence into the world – if man would make himself a chariot for God's presence but would receive no response – there would be no alternative way of revealing the *Shekhina*. The world would be void of the *Shekhina,* which would negate the entire purpose of creation. Indeed, God established this covenant with Israel after the sin of the golden calf, and it thus clearly pertains to the world's continued existence even after sin.

The emotional state of one reciting the Thirteen Attributes differs from that of a person in prayer, who falls upon his face and pleads to God. In prayer, the individual feels weak and helpless, broken and crushed – "A prayer by an impoverished man as he is faint" (Psalms 102:1). One who reads the Thirteen Attributes, in contrast, prepares himself to serve the role of a chariot for the *Shekhina,* to be the royal throne of the King of kings. On the one hand, this role expresses the greatness of man, who possesses the power to bring God's presence into the world; this is a majestic event, the crowning of the Almighty. On the other hand, it requires that the individual is no longer his own; he has entirely devoted himself to serving God by being His bearer in the world.

This act of sustaining the King's presence in the world poses a certain risk. Human beings might perhaps prefer to forego the Almighty's presence altogether. After all, if God is not present in the world, there is no punishment or demand of responsibility. From the pragmatic point of view, it is preferable not to call on God's name, to leave the *Shekhina* in exile.

In fact, this tendency is ancient in origin. The *Midrash Raba* (beginning of *Parashat Lekh Lekha*) comments that Abraham "*iḥa et hakera*" – he "mended the tear." The midrash later explains that the four kings who battled the five cities of the Jordan River valley (as related in Genesis 14) sought to harm Abraham, the one who "mended the tear" and brought providence back into the world, because they preferred a world without divine providence.

Calling on the name of God, on the Attributes of Mercy, means placing oneself into the King's hands. A person must approach this not with the hope of escaping, but rather out of a sense of responsibility and opportunity. He brings himself to judgment – and it is his hope that the judgment expresses compassion and grace, patience and abundant kindness.

Chapter One

"HaShem, HaShem"

In our introduction, we established that the concept underlying the recitation of the Thirteen *Midot HaRaḥamim* is that the *Shekhina*'s presence in the world depends upon human recognition. Hence, the presence of the *Shekhina*'s Attributes of Mercy depends upon the reading of the Divine names of Mercy by the servants of God. The general intent required when reciting the Thirteen Attributes is willingness to serve as the "chariot" for the *Shekhina*'s revelation. However, the precise meaning that we discover for each name adds an additional requirement of intention, not only regarding the meaning of the words, but also in terms of consciousness and awareness. We must comprehend what facets of God's presence we are bringing down into the world.

Ḥazal (our sages) conveyed a tradition that there are thirteen distinct Attributes of Mercy in these verses, although they do not enumerate precisely what they are; we must understand the difference between them and the unique significance of each in order to bring about their manifestation. In our studies, we will attempt to explain each attribute independently, basing our analysis on the comments of *Ḥazal* and the *Rishonim*.

The first attribute – or the first Divine name – is *Havaya*

(Y-H-V-H), which is known as the *Shem HaMeforash*, the Ineffable Name. (Because of the sanctity of this name, it is written and pronounced, outside of prayer, as "HaShem," "The Name." In the context of prayer, it is pronounced *"Ado-nai."*) The verse listing the Thirteen Attributes begins with a repetition of this name – *"HaShem, HaShem"* – and the *Rishonim* debate whether we count these two words as signifying two separate attributes, a single attribute, or no attributes at all.[1]

In the continuation of the Gemara cited in our introduction (*Rosh HaShana* 17b), the Talmud offers a different interpretation of each mention of the word "HaShem":

> This teaches that the Almighty wrapped Himself as a *shali'aḥ tzibbur* [leader of the public prayer service] and showed Moses the prayer service. He said to him: Any time Israel sins, they shall perform this service before Me and I shall forgive them. *HaShem, HaShem* – I am He before a person sins, and I am He after a person sins and repents.

Tosafot clarify the Gemara's intent and explain the significance of the use specifically of the name HaShem:

> Rabbeinu Tam says that the first two names are two attributes, as stated here: "I am HaShem before one sins, having compassion on him; and I have compassion after one sins if he repents." *"HaShem"* as an Attribute of Mercy differs from *Elokim*, which refers to the attribute of Justice.

According to Rabbeinu Tam's reading of the Gemara, *"HaShem, HaShem"* encompasses two independent and distinct attributes – compassion prior to sin and compassion following sin. This is not the only plausible read-

1. The view that only one attribute is signified assumes that the Thirteen Attributes must each be different from one another. Hence, the same word cannot signify two distinct attributes. According to the view that no attributes are signified here, *"HaShem, HaShem"* constitutes the introduction to the list of attributes, which actually begins with the word *"El."*

ing; the Gemara could have simply intended that *"HaShem, HaShem"* is one attribute that indicates that God continues to show compassion even after sin, just as He treats one compassionately before he sins. *"HaShem, HaShem"* would then imply, "I am God – I have not changed;" His single attribute of *Havaya* remains intact despite sin.

Indeed, Rabbeinu Tam's interpretation, while widely accepted, raises a number of questions. In what way does specifically the divine name of *Havaya* express an Attribute of Mercy? Moreover, why does the continued presence of this name despite a person's sin constitute a separate attribute, something different from its manifestation prior to sin? Indeed, if the persistence of this attribute after sin constitutes an independent attribute, we should seemingly add a second attribute to all the other *Midot* as well; God is *Raḥum*, "Compassionate," before sin and after sin, and so on.

Apparently, the fact that only the attribute of *Havaya* is repeated led Rabbeinu Tam to conclude that it is specifically the manifestation of this particular attribute after sin that reflects a new, independent attribute, even if it is expressed with the same term. Thus, our understanding of the difference between the two attributes depends upon how we understand the meaning of the attribute represented by this divine name. The explanation I will present is based on a discourse of R. Yitzḥak Hutner *z"l* printed in his *Paḥad Yitzḥak* (Rosh HaShana).

HAVAYA – GOD WILLS EXISTENCE

The simple meaning of the divine name of *Havaya* (literally, "Existence") relates to the notion that God gives existence to the entire universe; all of existence comes from Him. This is true not only in the sense of historical creation, but also in the sense that the very concept of existence is possible only on the basis of the will and power of God.[2] Nothing exists independently of Him; there is nothing whose existence is possible without the will of God. The very word "existence" can denote only God Himself or His will.

The existence that God did, in fact, will into being was built on

2. The Rambam presents this idea in the beginning of *Hilkhot Yesodei HaTorah*.

kindness – "*Olam ḥesed yibaneh*" (Psalms 89:3). What do we mean when we say that the creation of the world was an act of pure kindness?

Judgment, *din*, is impossible in the absence of the world. After all, "judgment" implies that a person receives what he deserves, that God repays each person in accordance with his conduct. Compassion and justice are responses to human action. Before the world's creation, there could be no such thing as a justified response, for there was not yet any situation that demanded one. The world's creation itself certainly cannot be a reward or response deserved due to a prior state, as there was no prior state!

In essence, this is the logic behind the Rambam's famous question regarding the reason for the world's creation. Creation, according to the Rambam, most certainly was not intended to meet any need of God, as He has no need or lack, nor could it have served to meet a need in the world, for the world did not yet exist. Therefore – without entering into the complex medieval discussion of this issue – we must conclude that the world was created through *ḥesed* – not as an act of justice and not in response to anything that occurred before the act of creation.

When someone gives his friend something he does not deserve, he has performed an act of kindness. When existence was given to nothingness, when everything was given to non-existence, this was the greatest act of kindness possible, one which is incalculable and beyond any conceivable quantification. Mathematically, we would say that the relationship between the existent and the non-existent is infinity; God's creation is thus infinite kindness. Thus, "The world is built through kindness."

According to R. Hutner, the attribute of *Ḥesed* inherent in the name of *Havaya* relates to this notion. God is the sole source of existence for everything – *Havaya* – and even before we evaluate that existence in any detail, we qualify it as infinite kindness in relation to the alternative – absolute non-existence.

This explains why the name of *Havaya* is the first of the Thirteen Attributes. *Havaya* relates to the bare fact of existence *per se*, and not any specific condition. Nothing in the world exists "more" than any other thing; as such, everything that exists receives the same degree of kindness from the attribute of *Havaya*. From the perspective of this attribute, there is no difference between adult and child, the wicked and the righteous, a bacterium and an elephant, or a worm and a human being. As it is not a response to any previous reality, the attribute of *Havaya* relates equally to every reality.

The subsequent attributes, in contrast, relate to particular situations; they are responses to human action. For example, the attribute of *Ḥanun* ("Gracious") is based on the verse, "I shall hear [the poor man's cries], because I am *Ḥanun*" (Exodus 22:26); it is manifest in response to the cry of the poor. Indeed, every other attribute is based upon the attribute of *Havaya,* the Almighty's will that there exist a reality outside of Himself. Only after we understand that God lends things existence do we note that everything in existence receives to a different extent, in accordance with what it deserves.

There are infinite different levels of power, beauty, and knowledge, and they express infinite and distinct manifestations of the attributes of kindness. *Havaya* is the first attribute of kindness because every other attribute is but a particular expression of the undifferentiated attribute of *Havaya.*

HAVAYA – GOD WILLS THE EXISTENCE OF SIN

This is the meaning of the first *Havaya* – "I am He before a person sins." What is the meaning of the second *Havaya* – "I am He after a person sins and repents"? The first attribute, signifying God's will that there be existence (and the lack of existence in the absence of His will), suffices only until the first sin, until twilight of that first Shabbat, when Adam partook of the forbidden tree. By definition, sin opposes the divine will, and God's will that there be existence does not include that which runs in opposition to His will. Thus, the existence of sin contradicts and annuls the creative act of the first attribute of *Ḥesed.* A world with sin – a world in opposition to God's will – cannot continue to exist by His will.

Thus, "I am He before a person sins, and I am He after a person sins." The second *Havaya* is a new attribute of *Havaya,* which includes even a world of sin. To put it more sharply, this is the attribute of *Havaya* that gives existence to everything, including sin itself. After sin, a person must be created anew, and God must sustain this new existence – an existence with sin.

Although the first attribute is perplexing, as we find it difficult to understand why God desired the world's existence in the first place, at least it does not cause utter astonishment. The second attribute, however, the attribute of *Havaya* after the sin, may initially leave us in a state of shock. God wants the existence of sin, as He wills the existence of a world in which sin is a component.

As we have noted, the reason that we recite the Divine Attributes is to turn ourselves into vehicles for their revelation in the world. In order to do so, we must have the proper understanding and intent when proclaiming each. The recitation of the first name of *Havaya* requires a sense of being entirely dependent upon the divine will, as existence has no meaning other than the will of God, who, in His kindness, grants life to all living things. The second attribute of *Havaya* has further significance and far-reaching implications both in terms of a general religious ethic and in the particular context of the *Seliḥot* recitation. The attribute of *Havaya* after sin is predicated on the fact that God wants the world even after sin; that He continues to give existence to a world that operates in opposition to His will. A person who sins "forces" the Almighty to consent to – and even grant existence to – the sin that he committed. When we utter the second *Havaya* in the *Seliḥot* recitation, we essentially ask the Almighty to support our sinful existence, to become a participant in the sin. What gall it takes to make such a request! Indeed, as R. Yoḥanan said, "Had the verse not been written, it would have been impossible to say such a thing!"

One who prays and recites the Thirteen Attributes after sinning must recognize that his conduct necessitates the involvement of the absolute Good in a world of sin, for without the Almighty's continued and boundless kindness, no sin would ever be committed. Kindness builds the sin and sustains it – and the sinner is responsible for the desecration of this pure goodness. One who sins not only betrays God; through his desire to succeed and continue existing, he defiles the divine good. There is an inherent, frightening contradiction in this regard. Kindness – the good seeking to bestow goodness – bestows goodness even upon evil, and thereby becomes a partner in its existence. The worshipper must accept responsibility for this before he can read the second attribute of *Havaya*, so that he can serve as a "chariot" for this attribute.

HAVAYA AND *TESHUVA*

The Gemara defines the second attribute to mean, "I am He before a person sins, and I am He after a person sins *and repents.*" Despite this stipulation of repentance, I do not believe that the second attribute of *Havaya* is reserved only for those who have already repented. First, God revealed this attribute after the sin of the golden calf, and the Torah does not describe any process of repentance on the *Benei Yisrael*'s part.[3] Second, the concept represented by this attribute – the world's continued existence even after sin – clearly holds true irrespective of *teshuva.* We see with our own eyes that unrepentant sinners continue to exist, despite the fact that sin brings an end to the first attribute of the world's existence. More generally – as we will discuss at greater length in subsequent chapters – all of the Attributes of Mercy, with the exception of the final one, apply before *teshuva* actually takes place.

R. Yoḥanan's intent, I believe, is that the Almighty tolerates sin in *anticipation* of *teshuva.* "I am He after a person sins" because he will repent at some point in the future. Why indeed does God's goodness extend to evil, to the negation of His will? Good sustains evil because the good believes that ultimately more good will grow from the evil through the process of repentance. The good believes in the ability of evil to rehabilitate itself, and this belief is itself part of the Attribute of Mercy inherent in the good.

The faith in the rehabilitative ability of evil, the faith in the sinner, is the added Attribute of Mercy of the second *Havaya.* "And God saw all that He had made, and behold, it was very good" (Genesis 1:31) – everything created in the six days of creation, represented by the first *Havaya,* was very good, because there was not yet any evil. There is another good, however, that had yet to be created – the good of repentance, which can exist only after the advent of sin.[4]

The second attribute does not contradict the first, despite the fact that the first attribute desires only goodness and the second wills even

3. Regarding the process of *Bnei Yisrael's teshuva,* see Appendix II.
4. Of course, God foresees everything, and He prepares the cure before the illness begins. This is why R. Ahava b. R. Ze'ira includes repentance among the things created before creation (*Bereshit Raba* 1:4).

evil. The second attribute desires evil because it knows that there is goodness even within the evil – the goodness of repentance. Fundamentally, then, the second attribute is reserved only for those who repent, insofar as its objective and ultimate purpose is *teshuva*. In actuality, however, *teshuva* is not a prerequisite for this attribute's implementation.

God, who is good, wants there to be human beings with free choice, even if they utilize their free choice for evil, because they can potentially utilize it for repentance and for good. This is an attribute of kindness, not of judgment. Judgment has no patience to wait until the future; from the perspective of judgment and strict justice, the future does not justify the evil of the present by offering the prospect of future goodness. One must experience a profound feeling of shame over the fact that he depends upon the second attribute to exist and that he did not succeed in actualizing the first attribute.

THE WILL OF GOD

The concept of the divine will appears here in two different senses. God wills the existence of the world, and God wills the existence of free will in Man. It follows that God, given that Man has sinned, wills the existence of the sinner, as well as the existence of sin and the evil implicit in it. However, it is obvious that evil itself is not the object and goal of God's will. In other words, God does not *desire* evil, even though its existence is included in His will – "Do I truly desire the death of the evildoer, says the Lord God; rather that he repent of his way and live" (Ezekiel 18:23). God's will, in this respect, means His agreement to the existence of something. Desire, on the other hand, refers to a goal to which His actions are directed.

This distinction illuminates a difficult passage in the midrash (*Bereshit Raba* 2:5):

> R. Abahu said: From the beginning of Creation, God perceived the actions of the righteous and the actions of the wicked, as is written, "For God knows the way of the righteous and the way of the wicked…." (Psalms 1:6). "And the Earth was *tohu vavohu*" – these are the actions of the wicked; "God said, 'Let there be light'" – these are the actions of the righteous. *But I do*

> *not know which of them He desires, whether the actions of these or the actions of these.* When it is written, "God saw the light, that it was good," [I know] that He desires the actions of the righteous, but does not desire the actions of the wicked.

How could the midrash ask which actions God desires more? Based on what we have explained, the meaning is clear. In the final analysis, there can be no doubt that God's will encompasses the actions of the wicked no less than the actions of the righteous; otherwise, they could not exist. The objective observer therefore questions which He *desires* more. When he encounters the verse, "God saw the light, that it was good," it becomes clear that although God wills evil, He does not desire it. The Creator supports the existence of both good and evil, but He is "on the side" of the righteous, and only their actions are desired.

This understanding has an important consequence for the way a person must recite *Seliḥot*. When reading the second attribute, one must do so with a willingness to repent; one cannot recite the second attribute while denying the possibility of *teshuva*. Although this attribute is effective even for one who at the moment stubbornly refuses to repent, it is simply dishonest and irrational for a worshipper read the name of *Havaya*, proclaiming the attribute of Compassion after sin, without at the very least a basic willingness to correct the wrong.

INTENT IN PRAYER

Let us now summarize the meaning of the first two attributes as they affect a person's intention as he prays.

When reciting the first attribute of *Havaya*, one should have in mind: "I call in the name of God who brings all the worlds into existence, and I request kindness because I exist; I am an object of divine kindness, and God desires the existence of all things. I do not request compassion on account of my personality, my conduct, the merits of my ancestors, or any other specific quality, but rather solely because through my existence I fulfill the will of God that the world exist, as expressed through the name *Havaya*."

Ḥazal suggest an additional explanation of the name of *Havaya*: "*Haya, hoveh veyiheyeh*" – "He was, He is, and He will be." In other words:

"You are He before the world existed, and You are He even when there is no world." This essentially expresses the same notion we have developed above, or, more precisely, the other side of the same coin. God is everything, and even before creation, He was whole and perfect. As such, I do not exist in order to satisfy a certain need, but solely because, in His absolute kindness, He wants there to be existence, even though that existence contributes nothing to Him. A person therefore cries from the very depths of his existence, from the inner, simple point that he exists: "*HaShem* – of whose will I am an object."

But the first attribute has an inherent limitation. It responds to the individual sinner, "You exist because of My will – but you are not in accordance with My will. You are not a reality that fulfills My will; how, therefore, do you exist?" At that point, we must proceed to the second attribute. When one cries out the second "*HaShem*" out of deep-seated feelings of shame and failure, he essentially says: "Indeed, I have failed and I have not fulfilled the divine will. Nevertheless, although I cannot understand how or why, You desire this, too. Even this receptacle filled with shame and humiliation, stained with sin – even this constitutes an object of Your will."

Of course, as mentioned, this is not possible without the prospect of *teshuva*. Somewhere in the back of one's consciousness, the seed of future repentance must already begin to sprout. "*Havaya Havaya*" has bestowed such abundant kindness for the sake of the world's existence that a sinner can "stretch" the divine will and even use it to protect himself, even with the sin still in his pocket, because he still has an opportunity to clean the stained garment.

Psychologically, there is a vast difference between the full process of repentance – including complete remorse for the past, a commitment for the future, and a thorough analysis of the vicissitudes of the soul – and a flickering of the willingness and desire to repent. Herein lies the failure of most of us; on Yom Kippur, we fail to proceed beyond the stage of willingness to perform *teshuva* and do not make the effort to correct our wrongs through *teshuva* itself. In any event, at the time of *Seliḥot*, we still have not reached the critical stage of rectification, but we have at least arrived at the spark of preparedness, raising the prospect of future repentance in order to justify God's anticipation. This spark must be part of our calling the second name of *Havaya*.

Of course, the tension that we have drawn between the first and second attributes deserves a separate, in-depth philosophical analysis. What is the relationship between God's desire for goodness and His desire for the world's existence? How do we reconcile God's desire for goodness with His desire that we have free choice? These are important questions that leading thinkers of many generations have addressed, but this is not our topic here. One who prays does not have to solve metaphysical, theological dilemmas. For him, it suffices to understand that both divine wills exist and that they are expressed in the first two Attributes of Mercy.

Chapter Two

El

The third of the Thirteen Attributes is *"El,"* a general term that simply signifies "God," referring to a divine being, both within Judaism and within other religions – including paganism. What is the connection between this reference to God and the quality of compassion or kindness?

Tosafot discuss the attribute of *El,* among other things, in their commentary to the Gemara about the Thirteen Attributes (*Rosh HaShana* 17b):

> *El* is the attribute of Strength, for with a mighty hand He prepares food for all His creatures, as it is written, "The lion cubs roar for prey, and to request their food from *El*" [Psalms 104:21].

It appears that *Tosafot* establish two concepts here, both of which complicate our puzzle. First, they identify the term *"El"* as a reference to strength and power, leaving us to wonder why this quality ranks among the Thirteen Attributes of Mercy. Second, *Tosafot* claim that this quality is most clearly manifest through God's provision of food to His creatures. Why does specifically this phenomenon exemplify God's unique power and might? Why not the shattering of stone or the overturning of mountains? Provision of food is certainly a great miracle worthy of admiration – but how does it demonstrate strength?

Tosafot's explanation is based on the literal meaning of the name *El*. In the *Shirat HaYam*, the song sung after the splitting of the sea, *Benei Yisrael* extol, "*Mi khamokha ba'elim HaShem*" – "Who is like You among the *eilim*, O Lord!" (Exodus 15:11). Rashi comments:

> "Among the *elim*" – among the strong ones, as in "and he [Nebuchadnezzar] took the mighty ones (*elei*) of the land" [Ezekiel 17:13], and "My Mighty One (*eyaluti*), hurry to my assistance" [Psalms 22:20].

In the verses cited by Rashi, the term *el* does not necessarily refer to a divine being; in his first example, the term "*elei ha'aretz*" clearly refers to strong human beings, not God. The Ramban similarly writes in his commentary to this verse that *elim* implies "*tokef veḥozek*" ("force and strength"). When the *Benei Yisrael* witnessed the manifestation of God's unparalleled might at the sea, they exclaimed, "Who is like You among the mighty, O Lord!" The pagans idolized all the natural forces; rain was one *el* and wind was another. All natural forces were viewed as powerful beings – but who among them can compare to the one, true God?!

God is called "*El*" because He brings together all the *elim*, all other forces. He is the "*Elokei HaElokim*," the powerful Being who exerts control over all other powerful beings. Thus, one of His attributes is Strength.

But as we noted, it is specifically from this perspective that it is difficult to understand why *El* is classified as an Attribute of Mercy. This name appears to denote neither mercy nor justice; "strength" is a neutral quality, through which God can have compassion on the Israelites trapped against the sea or visit retribution upon the pursuing Egyptian horsemen. The quality of *El* can serve the purposes of both justice and mercy.

Ḥazal instituted a special *berakha* to recite upon witnessing certain natural phenomena that remind one of God's might, such as cracks of thunder and bolts of lightning: "*Barukh shekoḥo ugevurato maleh olam*" – "Blessed is He whose strength and power fill the earth." I imagine that had I been standing on a cliff overlooking the Dead Sea when God rained salt and sulfur upon Sodom and Gomorrah, I would have recited this *berakha.* The display of power by God's attribute of Justice is no less impressive than bolts of lightning! If strength is associated with justice, why is it included among the Thirteen Divine Attributes of Mercy?

The Torah actually includes an explicit reference to *ko'aḥ,* strength, in the context of God's Attributes of Mercy. In the aftermath of the sin of the spies, Moses seeks to invoke the Thirteen Attributes on behalf of *Benei Yisrael,* and he introduces his plea by beseeching, *"Ve'ata yigdal na ko'aḥ HaShem"* – "And now, may *the strength* of the Lord be increased" (Numbers 14:17). The goal of the Thirteen Attributes is to achieve forgiveness, as Moses concludes, "You shall forgive our iniquity and our sin" (Exodus 34:9); in order to achieve that goal, Moses asks for a display of strength. Thus, there clearly is some connection between this attribute of *Ko'aḥ* and the system of divine mercy.

I would like to propose three levels of explanation, one within the other, of the place of strength in the context of God's kindness and compassion. These are not three alternative answers to our question; rather, each represents a deeper form of the basic answer.

FORGIVENESS REQUIRES STRENGTH

The very concept of strength in relation to God is somewhat perplexing. In the human context, strength is exhibited in the context of a difficult undertaking, the completion of which demands considerable effort beyond one's normal level of exertion. But with regard to the Creator and Master of the world, every undertaking is equally simple, for His word suffices to fulfill His will – as we say in our morning prayers, "Blessed is He who spoke and the world came into being."

When we apply the concept of "strength" to God, we refer to its perception by observers; that is, His "strength" is described as such only from the perspective of how it appears to man. Divine strength is demonstrated through phenomena that appear to us as unusual, impressive, and awesome. We do not recite the blessing *"shekoḥo ugevurato maleh olam"* over common phenomena, such as normal rainfall and ordinary winds, because we do not *experience* God's strength through them. When we witness lighting and fierce storms, on the other hand, the manifestation of divine strength is forced onto our awareness. These phenomena obviously do not entail increased exertion of effort on God's part; we rather relate to our *impression* of God's strength, which elicits the recitation of a blessing.

In contrast, the divine attribute of Strength – *El* – cannot refer to our impression of God's power. On the contrary, God's granting of forgiveness does not feature any impressive display; the nation will continue to exist just as it existed the day before, without any change in routine, or even, perhaps, in awareness. Moses petitions God to increase His actual strength because forgiveness – as opposed to earthquakes, wind, and fire – truly demands strength, in a unique sense of the term.

Implementing strict justice in response to sin does not require strength. As we explained in the previous chapter, the death of the sinner is a direct consequence of the sin itself, as sin, the deviation from the divine will, undermines the very basis of the sinner's existence. Sin disrupts the connection between natural existence and God's bestowal of life; ending the existence of sin does not require any action on God's part, but rather follows from inaction – "It is not the serpent that kills, but rather the sin that kills" (*Berakhot* 33a).

In the two cases in the Torah when these attributes are articulated – after the sin of the golden calf and the sin of the spies – Moses seeks to avert the nation's utter destruction. The people are threatened not with punishment, not even with death, but rather with the divine response of "I shall destroy them in an instant," the complete cessation of existence. Such annihilation does not signify strength; it is a natural consequence of sin. The mercy invoked in the Thirteen Attributes prevents this natural consequence.

Mercy does not entail avoidance of punishment, however. Indeed, after God declares to Moses, "I have forgiven as you said" (Numbers 14:20), He immediately proclaims the punishment that He will nevertheless visit upon the people – that the generation that sinned will not enter the land of Israel. Although annihilation appears to be a more extreme response than a lighter punishment, from the perspective of strength, it is actually much easier to implement. Punishment entails the sinner's continued existence despite his sin; this requires strength, as God must intervene to disrupt the natural condition, whereby sin equals nonexistence. When we speak of God's strength, we refer to the exertion of strength to oppose and overturn the natural process that God Himself established in creating the world.

This is illustrated in the second *berakha* of the *Amida* prayer, which *Ḥazal* call "*gevurot*," "strengths."[1] The phenomena noted in the *berakha* do not fit our ordinary conception of that quality. There is no mention of demonstrations of power or awesome might. In fact, a study of the *berakha* reveals that all of the phenomena it lists share one property – the reversal of a process that has already taken hold of a person. First, God is described as "*somekh nofelim*," who "supports the falling." When a person falls, he is seized by the force of gravity, which naturally draws him towards the ground.[2] But the Almighty, in His immense power, suspends and reverses the process – He supports the falling. A person falls ill and death has taken hold of his body – yet the Almighty intervenes to halt the process, because He is "*rofeh ḥolim*" ("healer of the sick"). A person is taken prisoner, without any possibility of escape – but he suddenly goes free, because God is "*matir asurim*" ("releaser of the bound"). The natural process flows in one direction, and God's might, His strength, overpowers it and sends it in the reverse direction. *Gevura* is an exhibition of *overcoming*.

God's attribute of "*Meḥayeh Metim*," resurrecting the dead, was selected to introduce and conclude this *berakha*, and supremely exemplifies *gevura*. After a person has perished, how can his life be restored? Death is final; there is no possibility of reversing this condition. While life leads inexorably towards death, death is not a basis for life. But the Almighty, in His infinite strength, overcomes this unidirectional process and resurrects the dead. God's power and strength signify that He overpowers creation and suspends His own rules.

This applies as well to the area of sin and forgiveness. Sin is death; this is the established law of nature. A person who transgresses resembles

1. As we have seen, *Ḥazal* use the terms *ko'aḥ* and *gevura* interchangeably, as in the blessing, "whose *ko'aḥ* and *gevura* fill the world."
2. From the perspective of *Ḥazal*, something that falls is to some extent considered already on the ground. The Gemara in *Bava Kamma* (17b) speaks of an article falling from a rooftop as a "broken vessel."

a *terefa* (a person mortally wounded), whom halakha treats as a *gavra ketila,* a walking corpse. One who lacks the foundation of existence is considered dead even if he still manages to breathe! Forgiveness, continued existence after and in spite of sin, entails the suspension of this law. God must overpower His world and suspend its laws – the laws that He Himself had imposed – in order to forgive. Thus, God's power is manifest specifically through forgiveness, and not through death.

Thus, to enable forgiveness, we appeal to God's strength – His ability to overpower the sin and the current condition of the individual in order to continue sustaining him and allow him to exist.

STRENGTH TO OVERPOWER GOD HIMSELF

The truth is that if the "natural law" that sin amounts to annihilation were comparable to other laws of nature, such as gravity, it would not require much "strength" to overcome it. Even if we claim, like the Rambam and against accepted modern science and philosophy, that natural laws reflect divine wisdom and truth, there is nevertheless no logical impediment to their suspension. God's will that the waters of the Sea of Reeds should stand as a wall does not contradict God's divinity, even if it constitutes a temporary deviation from the eternal divine wisdom. When God responds to our prayers and destroys our foes, as in the case of the instantaneous obliteration of the mighty Assyrian army (II Kings 19:35), we have no reason to say that this required a special degree of strength on God's part. The One who told water to lie flat can tell water to stand; the One who told oil to burn can tell water to burn.

Such is not the case, however, with regard to sin. One cannot say in the same casual way that He who told goodness to exist can tell evil to exist. The negation of evil is not simply the willful decision of God, which He can then choose to overturn, but rather is a law that reflects divine goodness itself. It is not a law of nature, but a law of theological morality. When we request forgiveness, we ask that the Good should sustain Evil, and this requires, as it were, a change in God's essence without God ceasing to be the absolute good. God is good, His will is good, and to exist means to be attached to good – but in order to sustain a person who sins, God must overpower the principles of goodness and act against Himself, as it were.

Compassion, in this instance, works against goodness; paradoxically, goodness subdues goodness. The goodness of compassion is the same goodness that stands unalterably opposed to evil – and yet, compassion leads the compassionate One to support the existence of evil!

This leads to a practical conclusion relevant to the intention and awareness required during prayer. When one asks for compassion with the divine name of *El*, invoking the attribute of Strength, he must be aware of the magnitude of the strength required. He requests not merely that a certain attributed should be employed, but that a divine attribute should be suspended. In order to have mercy, God must restrain His own attributes and overpower His goodness.

Ḥazal (*Berakhot* 7a) refer to this concept in the expression, "*sheyikhbeshu raḥamekha et ka'askha*" – "that Your compassion shall subdue Your anger." The term *kibush* ("subdue") is borrowed from the field of battle; the sages allude here to a kind of internal struggle waged among the Almighty's various attributes. "I shall annihilate them in an instant," which *Ḥazal* refer to here as "anger," is the original attribute. Compassion must "overcome" the anger, like an invader who comes to capture a city.

As we are drowning under the weight of our sins, we ask not that someone should take us out of the water, but rather that the water itself should support us. We ask God, who is good, to lift us, with the added weight of our sins, onto the waves of goodness. It is the good itself that drowns us – and we ask that the good now save us. Strength therefore expresses God's suspension of His own goodness. We turn not to God's existence to sustain us, but rather to His strength. We ask, "Act to sustain me, even though this attribute is in opposition to the absolute good."

An important component of God's strength is its temporary nature, and we must remember this when submitting a plea with this attribute in mind. It is meaningless to ask for continued existence in a state of sin, to ask goodness, "Accept me as I am now, in my present state, without judgment and without discrimination." This would be not a request for compassion, but rather a request for indifference.[3] God's

3. We will explore this distinction further when we discuss the attribute of "*Erekh Apayim.*"

permanent condition is one of goodness sustaining goodness; the use of "strength" signifies special effort, something out of the ordinary, an internal struggle, as it were, and assurance of this struggle's end must therefore accompany any request for it. It is inherently contradictory to ask that goodness disregard one's sin and condition of sinfulness; we can only ask God's Attributes of Mercy to allow us to exist temporarily, until we repent.

THE STRENGTH TO HAVE MERCY

Until now, we have explained why strength is needed for God to forgive and how strength is a critical component of divine compassion. But the attribute of Strength occupies an independent place in the list of God's Attributes of Mercy, indicating that strength *itself* constitutes an Attribute of Mercy, and not merely a means necessary to facilitate mercy.

In our attempt to explain the concept of "strength" in relation to God, we sought to identify a point of "difficulty" that required the use of strength.[4] The Aristotelian God is inherently perfect and has no purpose outside Himself. No strength is required in order to exist in that state, God's perpetual state of "rest," as it were. Strength must only be employed in order to achieve something new, to create instead of maintaining the *status quo* or actualizing the potential of what already exists. The divine decision to create a world outside of Himself and to achieve an objective outside of His perfection – regardless of the imponderable reason for that decision – requires the use of strength. Divine strength is creativity – creation *ex nihilo*, the creation of a world that had no existence whatsoever in that which preceded it.

The medieval Jewish philosophers, especially R. Yitzḥak Arama in his *Akedat Yitzḥak*, note that the system of divine justice is built into the nature of the world.[5] The *Akedat Yitzḥak* distinguishes between two different kinds of nature: a "blind" nature, the familiar laws of physics, and an "intelligent" nature, the laws of reward and punishment. According-

---

4. Of course, since God can never find something "difficult," the concept remains metaphorical.
5. The Rambam advances this concept to a certain degree as well in his *Guide of the Perplexed*.

ing to the first system, fire burns both the flesh of the righteous and the flesh of the wicked; according to the second system, fire consumes the wicked, but never harms the righteous. Accordingly, the reward of the righteous and the punishment of the wicked do not come from God *ex nihilo*, but rather grow out of the natural order, "something from something." We are not amazed by the fire produced from a match, and we similarly should not react with surprise upon seeing death for the wicked and life for the righteous.

The laws of "blind nature" are the four basic elements of the Greeks, the four basic forces of modern physics, Newtonian mechanics, or the laws of quantum physics. The laws of "intelligent nature" are the Thirteen Attributes of Mercy: "*Havaya Havaya*, Mighty, Merciful and Gracious, Longsuffering, and Abundant in Mercy and Truth." The continued existence of the *tzaddik* does not require the exercise of strength because it follows from "intelligent nature;" it is the existence of the *rasha* that requires creation *ex nihilo*, as it contradicts those very laws.

God's strength is necessary to sustain that which the laws of heaven and earth are incapable of sustaining; it enables a new creation of life despite the natural basis for its existence. The destruction of Sodom does not, from God's perspective, involve the exertion of strength, because the justice intrinsic in the world itself destroys Sodom. The kindness that spares the sinner comes from without; God's strength overpowers nature and creates something new. In this sense, strength is always an act of kindness, as creation is the quintessential act of *ḥesed* – "*Olam ḥesed yibaneh*."

Let us now translate this concept into the intention of the worshipper. When we call the name of *El*, we say that the world is deficient; it cannot exist according to the original system of creation. The world – at least my small world – does not justify itself and does not warrant its continued existence. It requires the exertion of power from the outside, an additional creation.

Imagine that a person purchases a new watch. After a bit of abuse, the watch stops functioning, and he returns to the watchmaker. The watchmaker explains that the watch is not defective, but its internal power source has been damaged. In order to function, it must be attached to a source of electricity; it cannot operate without power from an external source. This is precisely the situation of a person who sins. He has no basis for his continued existence, and thus requires additional power from an outside source – that is, from God. This is not because the human being is defective, but rather because by sinning, he has destroyed his internal power source. After sin ruins the divine creation, we must turn to the Creator – whose creation was destroyed due to no fault of His own – and ask that He provide that which is missing, to send a current of power that will enable us to exist.

What brazenness on our part! Strictly speaking, the "Watchmaker" should simply tell us to fix ourselves. But we tell Him, "The problem cannot be fixed, at least not right now, and You, the Creator, must ensure that it works anyway."

It is possible to make such a request because of God's covenant – "Had the verse not been written, it would have been impossible to say such a thing." The Almighty wrapped Himself as a *shali'aḥ tzibbur* and said, "I continue to create; I am the power source for the world, and not only its initial Creator."

The attribute of *El* includes three levels of strength – the strength to overcome creation, the strength to overcome the divine good, and the strength to create a constantly renewed existence, wherein the present does not have the power to ensure the existence of the next instant.

COMPASSION AND STRENGTH

We can learn an important, practical lesson regarding kindness from God's attributes – true *Ḥesed* entails consciously embracing the ideal of kindness and overcoming the opposing value of justice.

We tend to associate compassion with weakness. The common perception, which has its roots in Greek philosophy but is expressed in contemporary culture as well, views compassion as a person's emotional reaction, an effect rather than a consciously willed response. A person walking in the street naturally feels compassion for a crippled beggar; he does not decide to feel pity and help the poor man, but is rather compelled, forced against his will, by the emotion that overcomes him. He does not have the strength to walk past the man without helping, even if he so desires. He might think that had he only been stronger, more resolute, he could pass the beggar without assisting, but he is weak and overcome by his own emotions.

In fact, compassion is often associated with an image of softness, while lack of compassion is seen as tough and strong. We describe one who does not show compassion as if he *"hiksha et libo"* – "hardened his heart." The extreme manifestation of this perception leads to the preference for or admiration of the cruel, indifferent person, who acts as he sees fit without surrendering to compassion or taking into account emotionally influenced feelings of mercy and kindness.

The divine attribute of *El* teaches us that the precise opposite is true: strength manifests itself through the attribute of Kindness, through compassion. God's judgment is simple; it requires no proactive effort on His part, but rather only that He allow things to run their natural course. *Ḥesed* does not result from being overcome by an emotion; it is rather the overcoming of the attribute of *Din*. Having pity entails recognizing what is just, but acting differently – not because of fear or weakness or because one does not have the strength to follow strict justice, but rather because one has the strength to act kindly.

An act of kindness only fulfills the dictate of *"vehalakhta bidrakhav,"* walking in God's ways, if it involves a clear decision to suspend or restrain one truth – that of justice – in the face of another – that of compassion.

This is the meaning of the verse that *Tosafot* cited: "The lion cubs roar for prey, and to request their food from *El*." The lion cubs are strong, the kings of the animal world; they naturally – by justice – prey on the lamb. But sometimes, their power does not suffice to secure their prey, and they then ask to receive it from God, from outside the natural realm and the power latent within it. This is the attribute of Strength – the strength required to suspend the system of justice in the world and to grant kindness.

Havaya, the first of the Thirteen Attributes, teaches that, "The world is built through kindness."

Havaya, the second attribute, teaches that, "The world of sin is built through kindness."

El, the third attribute, teaches that, "The world of sin is built and sustained through the strength of the good to suspend justice."

Chapter Three

Raḥum and *Ḥanun*

The fourth and fifth attributes are *Raḥum* ("Compassionate") and *Ḥanun* ("Gracious"). There is no need to explain why these are included among the Attributes of Mercy, as their primary meanings clearly relate to mercy. This time, our objective is to understand the difference between the previous attributes, which are general names of God, and these two, which relate explicitly to the quality of mercy. Additionally, we must explain the difference between these two terms, *Raḥum* and *Ḥanun*.

THE WORTHY AND UNWORTHY OF COMPASSION

In their comment on the Gemara in *Rosh HaShana* 17b (the first part of which we have cited in previous chapters), *Tosafot* address these questions:

> *Raḥum* is also an Attribute of Mercy, but not like the attribute [*Havaya*], for there are different kinds of mercies, as it says [in the Gemara] here – before repentance and after repentance.

This comment does not provide an explanation for the term *Raḥum*, but simply proves that there are different kinds of mercy. Just as there are two distinct attributes of *Havaya* – one before the sin and one after the sin – the attribute of *Raḥum* differs from the three preceding attributes.

> *Ḥanun* likewise entails a different concept. For the attribute of Compassion [*Raḥum*] applies when it is not a time of crisis; before the crisis surfaces, He has compassion so that it does not surface. But *Ḥanun* means that He shows grace during a time of distress to redeem the one who cries out, as it is written, "He shall assuredly show you grace, in response to the sound of your cry" (Isaiah 30:19). This attribute means that, as it were, He is compelled to show grace even *unjustifiably* to the one who cries out, as it is written, "For when he cries out to Me, I shall listen [to the poor debtor's cry], for I am Gracious [*Ḥanun*]" [Exodus 22:26]. Meaning, despite the fact that you [the lender] received the collateral legally, for you lent him your money, nevertheless, you must return it to him, for if he cries to Me, the attribute dictates that I must heed his cry, because I am *Ḥanun* and I cannot bear to see his suffering.

These comments are intended to explain the unique significance of the attribute of *Ḥanun*, but a fundamental principle regarding *Raḥum* emerges from this explanation as well. Relative to the attribute of *Ḥanun*, the attribute of *Raḥum* is "*justified;*" there is a logic of compassion within the attribute of *Raḥum*.

We have previously explained that the first attributes relate to allowing existence to continue despite sin, without any distinction drawn between one creature and another. These attributes stem from the Almighty's commitment to sustain the world and maintain an existence outside of His own existence. *Havaya* and *El* relate to all existence indiscriminately, simply by virtue of the fact that something exists and God wants it to exist; they do not take into account any specific creature. In contrast to this concept of general existence, *Raḥum* relates to specific individuals, to each person on his own. At a certain point, the first attributes do not suffice – and it is then that the attribute of *Raḥum* comes into play.

As we emphasized in the previous chapter, mercy reflects truth no less than justice; it is incorrect to say that justice is based on reasoning while compassion is based on irrational emotions. Compassion also follows a certain logic, even if that logic cannot be easily described with clearly defined rules. We sense intuitively that some people deserve compassion more than others, and mercy may be justified or deemed improperly placed.

While strict justice relates exclusively to the transgression, without considering any other circumstances, the compassionate God takes into account all kinds of "mitigating" factors. An entire book would be necessary to enumerate the rules of compassion, to establish precisely which circumstances warrant compassion according to the internal logic of this attribute. In truth, one book would hardly suffice; as opposed to strict justice, compassion is subject to an infinite number of variables.

We are familiar with such a concept from modern-day justice systems. At the initial stage, a court convicts an offender based on nothing more than the facts of the crime. Thereafter, before the sentencing, claims are brought for the purpose of lightening the sentence. The judge hears the testimony of character witnesses and psychological assessments; he evaluates the defendant's family situation and considers factors such as whether he was subject to certain pressures, suffered a difficult childhood, or has contributed to society in other areas of life. After taking all of this into account, the judge reaches the decision of whether to lighten or even suspend the sentence. Two people may thus commit precisely the same offense but will receive different sentences because one is deemed worthy of compassion while the other is not.

According to *Tosafot*, the term *Ḥanun* refers to an Attribute of Mercy that is not based upon the rules, the logic that characterizes the attribute of *Raḥum*. Even after all the circumstances are taken into account within the framework of compassion, it is possible that the individual may still be deemed guilty and deserving of punishment. The sentence is issued and the punishment decreed for the offender; the first four attributes have not succeeded in overturning the decree, and he then cries out in distress and anguish. Even though divine justice and the expansive rules of divine compassion justify the punishment – even though the "collateral" was taken legally – there is another attribute that cancels the justified punishment. Because he cries out, God responds;

He is compelled, as it were, to show grace to one who cries out to Him – "I shall listen for I am gracious."

Raḥum entails the introduction of rational considerations that warrant pitying the sinner instead of punishing him. When claims in his defense fail to spare him, one is left with no option other than a plea to God invoking *Ḥanun*, which is not based on logical claims.

This concept underlies an additional explanation that *Tosafot* suggest for the attribute of *Ḥanun*, one that appears to be linguistically different but actually expresses precisely the same notion:

> The term *Ḥanun* also connotes an undeserved gift, as we say in *Berakhot* (6a), "I shall show grace to him to whom I show grace" [Exodus 33:19] – even though he is unworthy.

The Gemara in *Berakhot* associates the word *Ḥanun* with the root *ḥinam* ("free" or "undeserved"). The attribute of *Ḥanun* is extended to someone deemed "unworthy." The "worthy" here does not refer to someone who did not sin, since he would need neither compassion nor grace. The "worthy" one sinned, but deserves compassion; the "unworthy" one does not. "*Ḥanina*" ("Grace") involves an "undeserved gift" because *Ḥanina* comes after no basis has been found for *Raḥmanut* (Compassion).

We may thus summarize the first five Attributes as follows: *Havaya* gives existence to the world in accordance with the divine will, but when sin occurs, the initial will can no longer sustain existence. The second attribute of *Havaya* then dictates that God creates the world anew, for He wills the existence of the world even if it contains sin. But the existence of sin itself must then be sustained, and therefore the attribute of *El* "forcefully" sustains even the sin itself. But the sin endures, so the attribute of *Raḥum* assesses each creature and finds a reason to have compassion on some due to special circumstances, in accordance with the rules of compassion. But there are sinners for whom all the justifications run out; they are sentenced even after compassion is invoked. They deserve punishment until another attribute arises: "For when he cries out to Me, I shall listen – for I am gracious." The Almighty grants an "undeserved gift" to one who cries out to Him, and pardons his offense even without the justifications advanced by the attribute of Compassion.

THE NATURE OF GRACE

Let us now approach the attribute of *Ḥanun* in its own right. If indeed all excuses and justifications are insufficient to warrant compassion, why does God offer *ḥanina*? *Tosafot* explain that the cry of the poor man trapped in the mire of distress and retribution causes the attribute of *Ḥanun* to work on his behalf, without any valid reason. Why should a person deserve grace simply because he cries? Why should one who exercises inner strength and self-control, one who quietly endures the punishment rather than crying out from pain, not earn *Ḥanina*, while the hysterical person who erupts in tears as soon as the crisis befalls him deserves divine grace simply by virtue of his crying? After all, we are dealing here with God, not some human tyrant whose objective is to break the spirit of the condemned offender! *Tosafot* emphasize that God "has no choice" but to pardon the sinner. Divine logic does not agree to extend *Ḥanina*, but the cries of distress "force" God to do what He had already decided not to do! What, then, causes this attribute to go into effect?

In human experience, response to such a cry would be interpreted as a sign of weakness. I simply can no longer tolerate the crying, and so in order to free myself from it, I give in – not because I want to, but because I have no other way of sparing myself the ordeal of hearing the cries. Giving in to the tears and supplications of the accused would seem to be an example of the intellect of the judge being overwhelmed by his emotions, and hence an indication of weakness. Indeed, this is what led Socrates to refuse the advice to bring his wife and children to his trial in order to arouse the pity of his judges. He argued that it is improper to attempt to move rational judgment, an exercise in intellect and objective rational truth, by demonstrations of misery, which attempt to distort rationality and subject it to the power of the emotions.[1]

We already emphasized in the previous chapter, however, that the Divine Attributes of Mercy reflect strength, not weakness. God's attribute of *Ḥanun* must thus also stem from strength. But if so, why is the Almighty forced to show grace? Why is He compelled to act against His will?

1. It should be noted, of course, that the trial of Socrates resulted in his execution.

I would like to propose a solution, although with some trepidation, as we are entering the deepest and most mysterious realms of theological speculation. It seems to me that *Ḥanina* stems from the fact that the King of kings, the Creator of heaven and earth, identifies with His creatures, specifically with the human being, who was created in His image.

Imagine that I am angry at my computer because it does not work right. I disconnect it, and in response, it wails and shrieks. The computer's cries of anguish would evoke no feelings of pity whatsoever and would not deter me from proceeding with my harsh response to its wrongdoing. But when a human being cries, when a child wails after I have decided to punish him, I am incapable of bearing his pain, and I have no choice but to have pity. Why? The answer is simple: the human cry affects my heart because I sense myself in his cry. His cry reminds me – against my will – of what we share in common, and his pain therefore arouses my own pain. The cries of another person awaken the identification I sense with every other human being.

Indeed, this reflects an element of weakness; this response is based on my own suffering that results from sharing in another's suffering. But this "weakness" is a good quality, as it stems from sensitivity. This is a basic human quality – we sympathize with those with whom we identify. The joint human experience brings us into the pain of the sufferer and casts upon us the emotional and ethical need to alleviate the suffering. The only way to overcome this sense of identification – besides for shutting my ears entirely – is to harden my heart so that it cannot feel or identify with the source of the crying. This hardening of the heart would amount to sheer cruelty, even if would serve the purpose of justice.

Our feelings of sympathy and identification are extended to all human beings because we share the common experience of humanity. Can something similar be said about the King of the universe? I believe that we can indeed say that the Almighty identifies with His creatures for two reasons. First, He identifies with His creations because He created them; He invested effort into their existence. Second, and more important for our purposes, He identifies with human beings because they were created in His image and form, *betzelem Elokim*. Because man is created in His likeness, God not only has an interest in man, He is committed to a partnership with him.

The term *tzelem* ("image"), with respect to anything created, refers to the plan according to which something was made. The *tzelem* is the model, the work plans and technical specifications that describe the ideal which the item is intended to achieve. If a person is created in the "image of God," the human being has no other ideal or limiting specification other than God Himself. Every other creation is defined by its existence – a dog can never be anything more than a dog. But the human being is defined in the present through his potential in the future, and his potential is Godly – it is limitless. On the one hand, man is defined by what he currently *is*; but on the other, he is defined by what he can *become*, as the being that can infinitely transcend itself.

In relationships between people, mutual identification stems from the recognition that "There, but for the grace of God, go I."[2] God, in turn, relates to people with the approach, "There, by the grace of God, is someone who has the potential to be I, who can reach the Throne of Glory." Just as I identify with the crying infant or suffering adult because I can identify myself in his place, the Almighty identifies, as it were, with the person who sins and now finds himself in distress, because He identifies Himself, as it were, as the potential outcome of man's existence. It would be a vile sin and insane hubris were a man to see himself as God, but nothing prevents God, whose gaze encompasses the infinite, from seeing Himself in Man – "Had the verse not been written, it would have been impossible to say it."

After divine justice has convicted the sinner and after the divine attributes of Compassion have found no reason to show mercy and reverse the sentence, his cries out of suffering and torment arouse personal identification, such that the Almighty cannot, as it were, bear to see the person suffering. Even though punishment is warranted from the viewpoints of both justice and kindness, there is an additional attribute

2. Supposedly, the English evangelical preacher and martyr, John Bradford, uttered a variant version of this phrase – "There but for the grace of God goes John Bradford" – when seeing criminals being lead to the scaffold, a fate he did indeed eventually share when he was burned at the stake in 1555 by Queen Mary.

of Mercy that arises not between the judge and the defendant, but rather between brothers, as it were, with a shared existence. As a result of the cry, God is not only aware of the person's suffering, but also identifies with it; He senses it, as it were.

The process of judgment that we have described took place when the Jews were in enslaved in Egypt. When Pharaoh tormented *Benei Yisrael,* the Almighty was certainly aware of their suffering. He knew the facts and weighed them in light of the principles of justice and kindness. But when they cried out, "their pleas arose to God from the labor" (Exodus 2:23). At that point, "God heard their groans… God saw the Israelites, and *God knew*" (ibid. 24–25). The term "knowing" when used without an object refers to what we would call "feeling the pain." God "knew" in the sense of an inner feeling, just as "Adam knew his wife Eve" (Genesis 4:1).

This is precisely how God explained his decision to redeem the Jews to Moses (Exodus 3:7):

> "God said to Moses: I have surely seen the affliction of My people who are in Egypt" – *I am aware of the fact that they are suffering.*
>
> "And I have heard their cries by reason of their taskmasters" – *I have heard, I have felt, their suffering.*
>
> "For I *know* their pains" – *Now I know the pain and not just* about *the pain.*[3]

"Knowing" in this sense means being one with the object of knowledge.

3. This verse distinguishes between "seeing" and "hearing." "Seeing" refers to factual knowledge, awareness of the actual events, while "hearing" implies taking the facts to heart in a manner that arouses pity or identification, the "knowing" mentioned at the end of the verse. This is also the meaning of the statement of Joseph's brothers: "They said to one another, but we are guilty over our brother, when we say the distress of his soul when he beseeched us, and we did not hear; therefore this trouble has come upon us" (Genesis 42:21). We saw his distress, but we did not *hear*; we knew the facts in an intellectual manner, but we did not let his cries enter our hearts and arouse humane identification. This verse is the turning point in the story of the relationship of the brothers to Joseph, which revolves entirely around the question of estrangement and identification.

Benei Yisrael's cries affected a change in God's attitude towards them, for at that point, "God knew."

The same is true regarding everyone who cries: "For when he cries out to Me, I shall listen – for I am gracious." The attribute of *Ḥanina* entails God's identification and sense of oneness with the distress experienced by a creature created in His image.

Since justice is also part of the Good, punishment determined by justice and and ratified by *raḥamim* is also right and good, and from the objective perspective, the suffering caused by punishment is therefore justified as well. The subjective experience of suffering, however, is not good; it is evil. Even though the suffering is justified, the inner world of human experience is divorced from objective justice. The judge, sitting on the seat of justice, judges the accused externally. Neither the judge nor the judicial system take into account the basic humanity of the accused. The cry, the expression of suffering and pain, when it penetrates the ears of the judge, and from there settles in his heart, injects the personal, singular experience of the accused into the objective, rational considerations of the judge and awakens the man within him, the man who is brother, friend, partner, and equal of the defendant. The judge then finds himself facing the unredeemed evil of suffering, without justice to turn it into good.

Hence, the attribute of *Ḥanina* is triggered not by pain, the objective suffering, but by the cry, the subjective torment. It works through the ear, the hearing of the judge – "Then, when he cries out to Me, I shall listen – for I am gracious." If we were to describe the pain to the judge, so that he would *see* it with his eyes, he would judge and consider it objectively. *Hearing* indicates the internalization of the pain, converting it into the internal experience of the hearer, who is no longer merely an observer. *Ḥanina* is the response to the inner experience of pain, and not to the external knowledge of its existence.

Of course, as *Tosafot* write, it is only "*kivyakhol*" that God senses a person's pain, and "*kivyakhol*" that He cannot bear to see someone's suffering. Whatever the true, metaphysical explanation is, however, the basic concept is that of identification, knowing, a sense of oneness. "The Almighty wrapped Himself as a *shali'aḥ tzibbur*" – when we recite the Thirteen Attributes of Mercy, the Almighty is alongside us, the worshippers, and not on the other side, as the one listening to the prayers. God is part of the *tzibbur*, part of our community, for the recitation of *Ḥanun* because this is the attribute that equates us with Him, as it were. This attribute works because He does not judge our suffering, but rather shares in it: "*Imo Anokhi vetzara*" – "I am with him in distress" (Psalms 91:15). He prays, as it were, for the tribulations to cease, because He also, as it were, is affected by them. I am the criminal and He is the judge, I am the sinner and He is the forgiver – but when it comes to crying and distress, I am the sufferer and He, as it were, suffers with me.

This is a most profound concept in Judaism. Alongside the infinite difference and distance that separates God from man, we recognize as well God's identification with man. This is the concept of *tzelem Elokim*. We may debate the full meaning of this concept from now until eternity, but we cannot escape the basic point that this concept establishes: Man is not God, but he is made in the image and form of God. Man lives with the constant ambition and drive toward divine perfection, and this point leads to *Ḥanina*, an "undeserved gift." God shows "favoritism" toward those created in His image, as though looking out for His own best interests.

Even if the Almighty does not wish to lessen the *punishment*, as this would be unjust according to the rules of compassion, He nevertheless wishes to reduce the *suffering*, because all suffering is the suffering of the divine image, and God identifies with the sufferer and his suffering, as He is gracious. If it were possible to punish without causing pain, there would be no need for the attribute of *Ḥanina*. Because suffering is an inherent part of punishment, the attribute of *Ḥanina* must supersede the attribute of Justice, even when the attribute of *Raḥum* does not suffice.

If this is the correct understanding of *Ḥanun*, then it requires special intent as one recites this attribute in prayer. As we have noted, each attribute must be accompanied by an awareness on the part of the worshipper, based upon his role as the "chariot" bearing that divine name. According to the approach proposed here, one who recites the name of *Ḥanun* must cry out from suffering and torment, presenting before God the suffering in the world in a manner that arouses identification. Thus, the worshipper must also identify with the suffering; he must feel it, "know" it, and truly sense why God is "compelled" to alleviate the pain of the sufferer.

When a person declares that God is "*Raḥum,*" he says: "Look at the mitigating circumstances that arouse compassion toward my personal situation." But when he declares, "*Ḥanun,*" he says: "True, I have nothing to justify a lightening of the sentence. But please, our Father, it hurts me! It hurts!" When a child runs to his father after he has fallen, he does not think of all the logical reasons why his father should have pity on him. He simply cries out, and his father, with a primordial instinct, shares in his pain.

This quality must originate from the depths of one's heart, from the depths of one's suffering. It originates from the most simple and basic place within a person: I am not wise. I do not understand. I cannot have any sophisticated intentions. I just cry, "Ah!" To whom do we turn when we feel pain, if not to our Father in Heaven? And our Father, when He hears the cries of His children, of those who bear His name and His identity, cannot bear their pain and suffering: "Then, when he cries out to Me, I shall listen – for I am gracious."

Chapter Four

Erekh Apayim

The sixth of the Thirteen Attributes of Mercy is that of *Erekh Apayim* ("Delaying Anger"). What effect does this attribute have, and what is its precise meaning?

The Jerusalem Talmud, (Yerushalmi *Ta'anit*, end of 2:1), discusses this attribute at length. The Gemara begins by addressing the fact that this attribute is formulated in the plural form – "*Erekh Apayim*," as opposed to "*Erekh Af*:"

> R. Shmuel bar Naḥman said in the name of R. Yoḥanan: It does not say here *Erekh Af*, but rather *Erekh Apayim*; He delays His anger with the righteous and delays His anger with the wicked.[1]

The Talmud's formulation highlights a difference between God's patience for the righteous and His patience for the wicked. Indeed, for this reason some *Rishonim* count *Erekh Apayim* as two separate attributes within the thirteen.[2] This division would require us to differentiate between

1. This first part of the passage also appears in the Babylonian Talmud (*Eruvin* 22a).
2. As we mentioned previously, some *Rishonim* count "*HaShem HaShem*" as a single

the patience God extends to the righteous and to the wicked, to justify classification of *Erekh Apayim* as two distinct attributes. However, since we have adopted Rabbeinu Tam's view regarding the classification of the Thirteen Attributes, which considers *Erekh Apayim* a single Attribute, we will set aside this intriguing question.

The next passage in the Yerushalmi cites another comment in the name of R. Yoḥanan:

> It does not say here *Erekh Af*, but rather *Erekh Apayim*: He delays His anger before He "collects" [His "debt"], and once He has begun "collecting," He delays His anger and "collects."

The Yerushalmi refers to the Almighty's act of *geviya*, "collection," an analogy for God's anger embodied in the punishment that affects the individual. Whereas the previous attributes describe divine kindness working in opposition to divine justice, here, God's kindness works against "*Af*" – God's anger. The Yerushalmi continues:

> R. Ḥanina said: Whoever says that God is a *vatran*, that He yields – his intestines should be "yielded." Rather, He delays His anger and then collects what is His.

At first glance, it appears that this passage is meant only to reject a possible misconception. We might have thought that the Almighty "delays His anger" forever; R. Ḥanina therefore clarifies that this is not the case – God delays His anger for a long time, but in the end "collects what is His."

This is not, however, R. Ḥanina's intent. The fact that God "collects what is His" does not contradict or modify "He delays His anger"; to the contrary, it is the basis of *Erekh Apayim*. R. Ḥanina warns us not to think that *Erekh Apayim* means that the Almighty delays His anger because He is a *vatran* – that he does not care what people do. According

---

attribute, and some maintain that this phrase does not refer to an Attribute of Mercy at all. These *Rishonim* are compelled to find substitutes to complete the sum of thirteen attributes, and one possibility suggested is to divide *Erekh Apayim* into two distinct attributes.

to such a view, because of God's indifference, it is possible for Him to simply look the other way rather than react angrily to sinners, ultimately leading to a permanent suspension of punishment. But this is not so; the correct meaning of *Erekh Apayim* is that God "delays His anger and collects what is His." The two parts of this sentence are inter-dependent – God can delay His anger because He ultimately collects that which is His. The delay in anger does not result from disinterest or lack of concern – because God is a *"vatran"* – but rather because God knows that punishment is guaranteed, and He therefore has the luxury of waiting.

God cannot simply forego the divine attribute of Justice that demands punishment, which insists that the "debts" be "collected;" He is not a *vatran*. A human being hurries to collect his debts, as he is always concerned that he will not succeed in retrieving the funds tomorrow. God, on the other hand, is in no hurry; no obstacles will get in the way of collecting in the future.

DISTANCING ANGER

The Yerushalmi immediately proceeds to explain this concept: "R. Levi said: What is *Erekh Apayim*? He distances fury." R. Levi clarifies the meaning of the word *"Erekh,"* which ordinarily means, "extends." The phrase does not mean that God "extends anger," remaining angry for a long period without calming His rage; this most certainly would not be an Attribute of Mercy! Instead, R. Levi explains, *"Erekh"* means "Distances" in this context; the Almighty extends the distance between Himself and His anger so that the anger cannot be manifest, at least for the time being.

Onkelos similarly translates *Erekh Apayim* as *"Raḥik Ragiz,"* "Distances Fury," and this is, indeed, the simple meaning of this attribute. But what do we mean when we say that God distances His anger? How can we understand the concept of "distance" in the context of a divine attribute?

The Yerushalmi answers this question through the use of an allegory:

> A king had two harsh legions. The king said: If they live with me in the city, then when the citizens anger me, they [the legions]

> will rise against them. Instead, I will send them far away, so that if the citizens anger me, by the time I send for them [the legions], the citizens will appease me and I will accept their appeasement.
>
> Similarly, the Almighty said: *Af* [Anger] and *Ḥema* [Rage] are two destructive angels. I will thus send them far away so that if Israel angers Me, by the time I send for them and bring them, Israel will repent and I will accept their repentance.

The case of punishment described here is not one of a trial before a judge, wherein an individual commits a crime and receives the punishment warranted by the code of law. Here, we speak not of the cold objectivity of justice, but rather of *Af* and *Ḥema,* an outburst of rage in response to provocation. The king's anger surfaces as an instinctive reaction to the people's conduct, not as a calculated judicial decision. They are spared the results of that anger because some time remains as long as the legions have not yet arrived.[3]

Transferring this analogy to God and *Am Yisrael* (the people of Israel), a gap exists between God's anger and its repercussions. Yet there would seem to be a vast difference between the analogy and its application. In the case of a mortal king, there is always a gap between the decision and its execution because he is limited by the physical means at his disposal. Such a thing cannot possibly be said with regard to the Almighty, however, who "spoke and the world exists," whose word is its own execution. If God decrees, what holds back the immediate execution? If God is angry, why should there be any time lapse before the punishment?

This, then, is the special attribute of *Erekh Apayim.* This attribute drives a wedge between the Almighty's anger, the reaction of the attribute of Justice, and the punishment that should necessarily result from that reaction. Although God is angry and the anger smolders, you will not be affected by that anger because "He distances fury." We do not say that God does not grow angry at all, nor that He represses His anger

3. It should be noted that the scenario described in this analogy was not unfamiliar to the population of the Roman Empire; the unleashing of legions dispatched to ravage a country as punishment was a common phenomenon.

altogether, but rather, as is clear from the Talmud's analogy, that He distances the practical repercussions of His anger. The Almighty controls His anger and does not allow it to consume the sinner. Once again, we sense the strength entailed in the Divine Attributes of Mercy, as we saw when we studied the attribute of *El*.

What difference does this delay in punishment make? What does a person gain from the attribute of *Erekh Apayim*? After all, as we saw, God's *Erekh Apayim* results only in a temporary delay; eventually God will "collect that which is His." The Yerushalmi's analogy provides the answer – delaying the onslaught of the legions, the eruption of anger, grants the people the opportunity for *teshuva*. This attribute serves as a call for "appeasement," for repentance that will eliminate the cause of the anger at its root.

In this sense, the attribute of *Erekh Apayim* is similar to the second attribute of *Havaya*, which the Gemara states applies "after repentance." We can beseech the attribute of *Havaya* even before repenting because there is an expectation of ultimate *teshuva*. Similarly, *Erekh Apayim* acts before a sinner repents, but only because of the expectation of repentance.

The attribute of *Erekh Apayim* clearly does not grant atonement or forgiveness. The sin remains, as does the consequence – the impending punishment. Indeed, this attribute clearly does not give a person much relief, but rather should arouse anxiety and dread; God's anger may be postponed, but He is guaranteed to eventually "collect that which is His." Whoever says that the Almighty is a "*vatran*" – that "I have been saved, because He is not angry at me despite my sins" – is doomed because he will fail to use the delay to his advantage and utilize the opportunity to correct his sinful state.

The delay in punishment is merely a means through which the person can continue existing temporarily in the shadow of divine wrath. The legions are on their way and draw nearer each second; a person with attentive ears, sensitive to the ominous rumble beneath the soothing cover of *ḥesed*, will hear the dull beat of the marching boots as they make their way towards him and use the opportunity to appease the King through repentance.

"Whoever says that the Almighty yields – his intestines shall be yielded." If you think that you have not been punished because there is no anger, because God is indifferent and there is no Judge, then you essentially decree destruction upon yourself – for if God "gives in" to you, then He "gives up" on you altogether. As we have emphasized several times, there is no possibility of existing outside of God's will or against His wishes; if you are not an object of God's interest, you are not an object at all. The attribute of *Erekh Apayim* allows the sinner to exist despite the Almighty's angry look, but only for a brief period, until the legions arrive. Time is of the essence! The *Erekh Apayim* does not last forever.

JUSTICE AND ANGER

Note that anger differs from justice. Justice implies a trial administered by a judge who rules in accordance with the dictates of the law – a certain crime deserves a particular punishment. He must preside over the case in a controlled and disinterested manner, as it is his job to execute the objective truth of the law. Anger results when the offense is not simply objectively wrong but offends one personally. In fact, a judge who feels anger toward a defendant cannot be trusted to fulfill his role; anger reflects personal interest and should disqualify him from presiding over the trial. Anger is born only once we have left the realm of justice.

The attributes we have discussed until now worked in opposition to the divine attribute of Justice, whereas *Erekh Apayim* acts on the anger that develops subsequently. Accordingly, the attribute of *Erekh Apayim* goes into effect only after we have left the framework of judgment. This takes place with the advent of the previous attribute of *Ḥanun*. As we explained in the previous chapter, *Ḥanun* comes into play once the sentence has already been issued and all avenues within the realm of judgment have been tried. A person's cry then arouses the Creator's personal identification with His creation, and the eternal, transcendent God identifies with the creature made in His image. The stage of *Ḥanina* entails the neglect of the attribute of Justice as a result of God's "personal interest" in His children. For this very reason, the next stage is a situation of anger.

Once God looks upon the person from the perspective of personal identification, the response to a sinner is naturally one of anger, as though God takes personal offense. If the Divine image commits a sin, he has slighted God. God sees, as it were, the *Shekhina* being ruined and sanctity desecrated. He no longer views the sin from the calculated perspective of the judge, without any personal interest in the result, for I cried out to Him: "Then, when he cries out to Me, I shall listen – for I am gracious." The success of the previous Attribute gives rise to the need for the next. Thus, anger is, at its root, an Attribute of Mercy; the fact that God "collects what is His" is included in the Attribute of Mercy of *Erekh Apayim*.

The philosophically sophisticated will wonder if I am suggesting that God actually takes personal offense or feels real anger. I leave that matter to the great Jewish metaphysicians, the Rambam and R. Hasdai Crescas. When a man is pleading for his life, desperate and terrified, he has neither the need nor the possibility to construct philosophical theories about passions and intellect in the Divine Being. *Ḥazal* attribute anger to God, and whatever the philosophical explanation is, this means that the human being's actions arouse within Him an emotional response that is warranted in light of the personal offense. As it were, God looks upon the sinner and erupts in a rage of fury because His image, the *tzelem Elokim*, has been desecrated.

The Yerushalmi emphasizes specifically in this context that "Whoever says that the Almighty yields – his intestines shall be yielded." After the attribute of *Ḥanina*, there is no longer any possibility to consider that the Almighty will simply relent – not after we cried out to him and demanded that He see within us the divine image, the "chariot" for the *Shekhina*, the potential for the existence of Godliness in the world. Without God's personal identification, we would never pass the stage of *Ḥanina*, but that same concern results in anger – and God will certainly "collect what is His." He will demand a personal accounting because I have offended His personal image. The only option is to accept God's angry, threatening closeness and to try to correct the mistake through repentance.

When we proclaim that God is *Erekh Apayim*, we beg Him to delay that response, to grant us the right to live amidst the anger and fury until *teshuva* is achieved. "You, my Father and King, are angry, and I accept this and acknowledge the reason for this anger. My existence was intended to serve as an image of God, and I betrayed this purpose.

Yet, amidst this anger, I hang my hopes on the opportunity You will grant me to appease You, for You are *Erekh Apayim*."

This, I believe, is how we should understand the plural form of *Apayim* (without interpreting the phrase as indicating two separate attributes). As we have noted, divine anger is fundamentally a positive attribute, an indication of God's identification with the person, His closeness and love. God delays His anger to both the righteous and the wicked. He is *Erekh Apayim* towards the righteous because He wishes to give him the opportunity to serve once again as a "chariot" for the *Shekhina*. The sinner offers no such hope, but his chance for survival hinges on the attribute that suits the righteous, the *Erekh Apayim* that results from the potential of *teshuva*. He must therefore accept the inevitable "collection of what is His," for God is not a "*vatran*" towards those He cares about. The sinner who appeals to *Erekh Apayim* is knowingly exposing himself to God's anger in order to buy time for appeasement.

As we saw, both the *Targum Onkelos* and the Yerushalmi translate the term "*Erekh Apayim*" as "Distances Fury." We proved from the Yerushalmi's analogy that distancing anger does not eliminate anger; the anger exists and continues to approach. I believe that we may propose another explanation of this term that will enhance the picture we have drawn of this attribute.

Why does the word "*af*" (literally, "nose") signify anger? The common explanation is that the word is meant to recall the image of an angry person, who breathes heavily; his nostrils flare, thus giving the impression that the anger exits from his nose. I would like to suggest that the term *af* relates to the first stage of the exhibition of anger – the long, deep intake of breath that precedes the eruption of rage. One who has been angered fills his lungs with air and actually inflates himself with anger; soon enough, the pent-up fury bursts forth.

Accordingly, the term "*ma'arikh af*" means prolonging this deep breath. The Almighty delays the outburst of anger and prolongs the process of accumulating rage.

This interpretation clarifies and elaborates on the qualities of *Erekh Apayim* that we have already revealed. The stage of *Erekh Apayim* does not eliminate the anger, but rather delays it – moreover, it actually intensifies it! According to this explanation of *Erekh Apayim,* there is no way to ignore the sound of the impending legions, for the longer they take to arrive, the stronger they become. The delay is, in fact, simply the preparation of the anger. If you are not wise enough to appease the King before the legions arrive, this delay will not only have been for naught, it will have had the effect of creating an especially forceful rage that will eventually overcome you.

DISTANT AND IMPRISONED ATTRIBUTES

The continuation of the Yerushalmi's discussion of the analogy of the king's legions can help us understand how the delay in anger comes about. The Yerushalmi presents two images to illustrate the delay of punishment. The first involves distance: "The Almighty said: *Af* and *Ḥema* are two destructive angels. I will thus *send them far away.*" R. Yitzḥak then adds a different image:

> R. Yitzḥak said: What is more, He locked them [the destructive angels] away. This is what the verse means, "The Lord has opened His treasury and taken out His instruments of fury" (Jeremiah 50:25) – by the time He goes through the trouble of opening [the treasury], compassion arrives.

What does R. Yitzḥak add to the original understanding through his introduction of a slightly different analogy? What is the difference between distant legions and legions that have been locked away, other than another few minutes of delay? And what is the implication of this difference with regard to the application of the analogy to the Almighty and His anger?

In order to answer this question, we must explore what it means to "distance" or "lock away" a divine attribute. What do we mean when we say that some attributes are "near" to God while others are "far" from Him?

The Creator's relationship with the world is based upon goodness and His desire to perform goodness. Benevolence and kindness flow directly from goodness, because, in the words of R. Hasdai Crescas, "The nature of the Good is to do good" ("*Teva HaTov lehetiv*"). All of God's attributes must thus stem from good. Anger, God's demand to "collect" His "debt," is justified only in that it ultimately serves the purpose of goodness; it is a means of goodness.[4] Conceptually, then, the attribute of anger is evil, but it joins the Good only to serve it. Anger operates on the level of "*bediavad;*" it is a *yerida letzorekh aliya* ("descent for the purpose of ascending").

The Yerushalmi's image of "distance" between God and His legions expresses this quality of anger. Although anger is one of God's attributes, it is nevertheless a "distant" attribute, one that the Almighty utilizes only after the "near" attributes have failed to achieve the desired result.[5] Anger is a borrowed attribute, a means of the good, because is sustains the individual until he repents, but a certain contradiction between goodness and anger remains because anger contains an element of evil. In the Yerushalmi's analogy, this disparity is described as the "distance" in time between the king and his legions, the delay before God expresses His anger.

The "distance" explains the basis of the delay; when God enlists the services of an alien element rather than expressing grace from within the internal divine good, the response is slower because it pains God, as it were, to use this method. If the Almighty brings me near, that is kindness; if He pushes me away so that I can eventually draw near, that is justified and ultimately good, but it entails releasing the forces of evil and destruction. Even when a father realizes that he must administer punishment for his child's own good, he turns his head to the side; he does not hurry to inflict the necessary pain. God's response is similarly not immediate; God delays it, a little bit and then a little bit more, hop-

4. This point is noted by the medieval philosophers in their discussion of the question of how the Almighty punishes the wicked. The Ralbag claimed that the rule of "nothing bad comes down from the heavens" applies even with regard to the suffering of the wicked; punishment – pain and suffering – is bad. R. Hasdai Crescas' response was that evil which serves the good – such as punishment – is also good, and can thus be included among the attributes of God.
5. It is notable that just as ethicists from King Solomon to the Rambam to contemporary *ba'alei musar* have advised distancing oneself from anger as much as possible, this is the "divine ethic" as well. Although anger is necessary, it is far from being a natural attribute within the framework of divine goodness.

ing that in the meantime the sinner will repent and avoid punishment. This would allow the Almighty to act in the preferred manner of love and forgiveness, rather than in the *"bediavad"* manner of cruelty and anger.

What does the image of "locking away" add? Since anger contains an element of evil, it entails – at least from the perspective of *"lekhatḥila,"* the preferred way of doing things – a diminution of the perfection and purity of God's love and grace. As such, God encounters, as it were, some "difficulty" in utilizing anger. The anger is locked away; it is not readily available for use. Until the final decision is made to use it, anger does not even appear on the list of options. Given the impropriety of anger and the apparent inherent contradiction between it and divine goodness, it does not stand before God as an attribute until there is no other option than to search for it. As it were, as long as the Almighty is not angry, He is not capable of anger! The attribute of Anger is not possible until it becomes necessary.

R. Yitzḥak does not offer a differing view, but rather deepens the same basic idea. The concept of "distance" expresses the fact that anger operates on the level of *"bediavad"*; the image of "locked away" teaches that it is rejected. The Almighty is filled with anger, but He delays the outburst because anger is a foreign attribute – and, moreover, an attribute that contradicts His goodness. Until He decides to access this attribute, until He girds Himself with this attribute that does not at all suit Him, the possibility remains that compassion will prevail, that the sinner will repent and appease, that he will calm the rage and eliminate its underlying cause.

Students of the Rambam will once again surely object that all of God's attributes are one and the same with His essence. He and His compassion are one; He and His anger are one! They are presumably correct, but it nevertheless seems that being one with the attribute of Anger is something that God does not deem worthwhile to do. Until He is angry, until anger becomes an attribute like God's other attributes – "by the time He goes through the trouble of opening" – there is time for repentance.

When a person sins, he does not merely receive a "bad grade;" he causes anger in the One who expected achievement from him. Sin is not only a failure, but also an affront to the sanctity of the Creator in whose image we were created, and anger results. But the Almighty delays and distances anger to the furthest extent possible, without eliminating it – not because He does not want to eliminate it but because it cannot be eliminated. Out of this tension – the delay of anger together with its urgency – an opportunity arises for us to repent. *Teshuva* can eliminate the anger (or, in the Yerushalmi's words, can "appease") after mercy succeeded only in delaying it. Therefore, the attribute of *Erekh Apayim*, in the mindset of the worshipper, must include an existential feeling of God's smoldering anger – and the glimmer of hope for *teshuva*.

Chapter Five

Rav Ḥesed

The seventh of the Thirteen Attributes of Mercy is "*Rav Ḥesed*."

What is the meaning of the word "*Rav*" that is appended to the word "*Ḥesed*" in this phrase? It is possible, on the level of *peshat* (the straightforward reading of the verse), that "*Rav*" here should be understood to mean "Master," such that *Rav Ḥesed* would mean "Master of Kindness." Alternatively, we could interpret "*Rav*" as a verb meaning "Does in Abundance," in which case *Rav Ḥesed* means that God performs *ḥesed* in greater abundance than other attributes.[1] However, in the Gemara in *Rosh HaShana* (16a), *Ḥazal* offer a different interpretation for the word "*Rav*" in the course of a discussion of the Day of Judgment (of the End of Days, according to Rashi):

> Beit Shammai say: There will be three groups on the Day of Judgment – one of the completely righteous, one of the completely wicked, and one of those in the middle. The completely righteous are immediately inscribed and sealed for eternal life; the completely wicked are immediately inscribed and sealed for *Gehinom*

1. See, for instance, the commentary of the Ramban.

> (*Hell*). As it says, "And many of those who sleep in the dust shall awaken – some for eternal life and some for disgrace, for eternal abhorrence" [Daniel 12:2]. Those in the middle (*beinoniyim*) descend to *Gehinom*, cry out, and then ascend… Regarding these people, Hanna said, "The Lord puts to death and revives; casts down to the underworld and raises up" [1 Samuel 2:6].
>
> Beit Hillel say: *"VeRav Ḥesed"* – *mateh kelapei ḥesed* (He tilts toward kindness).

It is clear from the Gemara's presentation that Beit Hillel's interpretation of *Rav Ḥesed* is a response to Beit Shammai's view concerning the *beinoniyim*. Beit Shammai maintain that the *beinoniyim* descend to *Gehinom* and then rise, whereas Beit Hillel disagree, contending that God "tilts toward kindness" for this group – they avoid *Gehinom* through the attribute of *Rav Ḥesed*.

Rashi explains Beit Hillel's metaphor: "Tilts toward kindness: Since they are equally balanced [between sins and merits], He tilts the decision toward merit, and they do not descend to *Gehinom*." The Gemara's formulation is based on the image of a set of scales with two arms, one holding a person's merits and the other containing his demerits. In the case of the *beinoni*, the two sides are perfectly balanced, without one weighing down the other. In such a situation, according to Beit Hillel, the Almighty employs the attribute of *Rav Ḥesed* and forcefully tilts the scales down to one side.

The word *"mateh"* ("tilts") in the context of judgment is jarring, as it brings to mind the explicit prohibition in the Torah, *"Lo tateh mishpat"* – "Do not distort a judgment" (Deut. 16:19). Moreover, the image of tilting scales brings to mind the prohibition of cheating in the marketplace through faulty weights and measures – "You shall have just scales and just stone weights" (Leviticus 19:36). Indeed, the attribute of *Rav Ḥesed* means just that – "illicitly" tilting to one side and thereby disrupting the balance. God "weighs" all people on earth, and the wicked are sentenced to *Gehinom* as a result of the scale's determination, but when it comes to the *beinoniyim*, God overlooks the scale's precise measurement and decides in favor of kindness. At first glance, this attribute seems to entail an element of falsehood and distortion of justice. What is the underlying basis that allows for this "tilting" of judgment?

TILTING THE SCALES

R. Hutner directs our attention to the state that led to this "tilting" – the balance between good and evil in the *beinoni*. We obviously do not know the accounting of our mitzvot and sins, nor can we identify the precise weight of any given mitzva or transgression. But the fact that the Gemara describes the situation of a *beinoni* in this manner demonstrates that such an accounting indeed exists and is known to God. Sins and merits are subject to arithmetic, such that there can be a situation of an exact balance between them; the ethical value of a good deed equals and is balanced by the ethical weight of the bad.

More broadly, R. Hutner asserts, the equality of the values of good and bad shows that good and evil are actually equally represented in this world. The Almighty created the world on the basis of the fundamental concept of free will (*beḥira ḥofshit*); in order to maintain it, good and evil must be two equally possible choices available to the chooser. The metaphysical weight of the good and the evil must be equal in value, so that the choice of man not be weighted in advance towards one side.

Despite this equal balance, the Rambam (*Hilkhot Teshuva* 7:5) codifies a tradition that good is guaranteed ultimate victory in the struggle between good and bad:

> All the prophets commanded repentance, and Israel will be redeemed only through repentance. And the Torah has already guaranteed that Israel will ultimately perform repentance at the end of their exile, immediately whereupon they will be redeemed, as it says, "It shall be when all these things come upon you ... you shall return unto the Lord your God ... And the Lord your God shall restore ..." [Deut. 30:1–3].

R. Hutner explains that this guarantee of ultimate repentance constitutes an exception to the precept of *beḥira ḥofshit*, a breach in the balance between good and evil that is entailed by the concept of free will. Free will is, in fact, not absolute; from the very outset, the world's Creator guaranteed a tipping of the scales between good and evil, and good will, in the end, weigh down evil. We live in a balanced world, but underneath the veil of day-to-day existence lies the ultimate triumph of good. Only in the future will we see this advantage of good over evil, but it must already exist in the present if its future expression is guaranteed.

R. Hutner claims that this is the attribute of *Rav Ḥesed*. In judgment, in the law governing creation, evil is precisely equal to good, but in the world of *ḥesed*, a certain measure of good has a greater value than the same measure of evil. They are equal – but not entirely equal. The possibility thus exists of a balanced scale, with the two sides perfectly equal, that tilts in favor of kindness – because goodness is worth more.

How can two equal entities not be entirely equal? How can there be an exception to free will, if the entire value of a mitzva stems from the fact that the individual chose to do it with his *beḥira ḥofshit*?

The answer emerges from the verse in which the Almighty presented free will to His people: "Behold, I have placed before you today life and goodness, and death and evil" (Deut. 30:15). On the one hand, the human being chooses between two equal values – good and bad. But at the same time, the truth is that this is also a choice between life and death, between existence and nonexistence, between something of worth and sheer nothingness. The concept of free will requires that the Almighty present us with two possibilities as though they exist in equal measure, but from the divine metaphysical perspective, no such choice exists; the good is God – existence – while evil is the absence of existence, nothingness, the nonexistent. Goodness is God, and evil is thus the absence of God.

This tension led many philosophers to dualism. In order to ensure complete and meaningful free choice between good and evil, they concluded that evil is also an expression of a divine existence; there is a good god and an evil god, and you must choose between them. In fact, the idolatry known to the Talmudic sages in Babylonia was a dualistic idolatry that believed in a struggle between divine good forces and divine evil forces. The apprehension that this conception could infiltrate Judaism lies behind the warning of R. Zeira (*Berakhot* 33b), "One who recites "*Shema Shema*" should be silenced," as it appears as though he accepts the existence of two deities. In contrast, we affirm that "the Lord our God – the Lord is one." Since God is one, good is divine and evil is nothing. Evil is found only in a place that is not filled with the divine light, a place that we have not filled through the selection of good. Hence, where goodness is absent, it appears to us that there is evil.

The choice between chocolate cake and cheesecake for desert is a free-willed decision, but not one that involves values; the two possibilities are perfectly balanced. When it comes to the choice between good and evil, however, there is a right answer, a morally compulsory response. The choice of good is both free-willed and value-based; a person chooses goodness because it is right and proper. Through his own free will, the individual recognizes the ultimate truth – that goodness is God and evil is bad and valueless.

The choice, then, is indeed free – but it is the freedom to choose that which is logically and necessarily true. It is the response of a man that affirms that the truth is true, or, more precisely, the response through which he adopts the objective truth as his own personal truth. It is the submission of the subjective to the objective existence of God.

This is the basis of the attribute of *Rav Ḥesed*. When a person chooses evil, he is guilty in equal measure to the merit he earned through the goodness he chose earlier. In the world of the human being, his merit and demerit are equivalent, and the gates of eternal life are therefore closed to him. However, in the world of the Almighty, in the world of the Master of *ḥesed*, good is always worth more than evil. God therefore tilts the scales in favor of kindness – and the individual thereby earns his share in eternity.

It follows that in the natural world of creation, there is no place for the attribute of *Rav Ḥesed*, which subverts and contradicts the principle of free will based on the perfect balance between good and evil. In the world of the Creator, however, this attribute expresses the absolute existence of God, who is wholly good. Hence, the operation of this attribute is an invasion of our world by the divine world, the subjugation of our world to the absolute divine goodness. In the ideal world, man would enthrone Truth in this world through the operation of free will, but this attribute abdicates that goal and transfers power to He who is Master of Mercy and Truth.

According to Beit Shammai, God's mercy guides the *beinoniyim* to *Gehinom* in order to then rise from there to eternal life. According to Beit Hillel, however, God's mercy disrupts the basic equilibrium of justice upon which the realm of *beḥira ḥofshit* rests in order to deliver the *beinoniyim* straight to *Gan Eden*. As far as the rules of judgment are concerned, the *beinoni* should be sentenced neither to *Gehinom* nor to *Gan Eden*, as he neither ascends nor descends on the "scale," but God's kindness searches for a way to bring him to eternal life.

The balance that underlies free choice cannot be eliminated altogether, for then the justification for the world's creation would collapse. For this reason, the attribute of *Rav Ḥesed* cannot save the wicked (although other attributes might). The *rasha* is subject to the consequences of *beḥira ḥofshit*, and he bears accountability for his actions. However, when justice's verdict remains undecided, as in the case of the *beinoniyim*, there is room for kindness to save them.

SUPPRESSING SIN OR RAISING MERIT

After establishing that God "tilts toward kindness," the Gemara proceeds to ask a technical question: "*Heikhi avid*" – "How does He do this?" What causes the transition from the verdict of a world of free choice to the verdict of a world of *ḥesed*? The two worlds appear contradictory. What has changed during the weighing of merits and sins? The Gemara offers two answers:

> R. Eliezer says: He depresses ("*kovesh*"), as it says, "He shall again pity us, He shall subdue ("*yikhbosh*") our iniquities" [Micah 7:19].
>
> R. Yossi ben R. Ḥanina says: He lifts ("*noseh*"), as it says, "who bears iniquity and forgoes ("*noseh*") on transgressions" [Micah 7:18].

Rashi explains these two answers according to the imagery of the two sides of the scales. According to R. Eliezer, "He depresses the merit side of the scale, and the merits weigh down the iniquities;" God makes the merits appear to weigh more. According to R. Yossi, "He lifts – He raises the iniquity side of the scale," so that the demerits appear to weigh less.

At first glance, this discussion seems almost humorous. If we were dealing with an unscrupulous merchant in the marketplace, we might point to the two ways in which he could manipulate the scales to defraud customers – he could either place his hand on the side of the scale with the merchandise, so that it *actually* weighs more, or he could place his hand underneath the counterweight and raise it, so that the merchandise will *appear* to weigh more. But what is the meaning of this allegory in reference to God? How does a crooked merchant's different schemes to cheat his customers reflect upon God's "tilting" of the scales weighing good and evil?

I suggest that we understand the metaphor almost literally. Essentially, this is a graphic and daring description of our explanation of God's "tilting" of the scales. R. Eliezer maintains that God adds the weight of His hand to the side of merits; while one side of the scale holds demerits, the other side holds merits as well as the added "weight" of God. On the side of my merits, alongside my good deeds, there is something extra – the presence of the *Shekhina* itself. The good I perform does not simply resemble divine goodness – it is Divine Goodness itself. My good deeds, the actions I performed that created goodness in the world and through which I have drawn closer to God, are themselves the presence of the *Shekhina*; they themselves constitute *kedusha*. The process of striving for perfection and self-transcendence through one's own free will is a reflection of absolute perfection, and every act of goodness performed by a human being therefore has the additional value of the *Shekhina*, of sanctity.

Thus, although good and evil are equal in weight from the perspective of the actions themselves, nevertheless, with respect to the end result, good always weighs more than evil. The scales of the *beinoni* are always tilted in favor of kindness and goodness because God has added Himself to the side of the merits, outweighing the side of sin.

This is, in fact, the concept that underlies the entire recitation of the Thirteen Attributes, during which we position ourselves to be a basis and "chariot" for the *Shekhina*. This willingness is itself an act of goodness, but beyond the merit I earn for my attempt, I earn merit as well for my success in serving as this chariot, for the weight of the entire chariot, including the One riding it, exceeds the weight of the mitzva act itself. Thus, a cycle emerges: the one who recites the attribute of

Rav Ḥesed, who carries this name, at the same time produces the basis for that attribute's effect.

R. Yossi ben R. Ḥanina presents us with a different image. God lifts – He raises the side of the scales holding the iniquities. The explanation is clear, although the pen trembles a bit in writing it. When a person commits a transgression, he bears full responsibility for his action; the scale of iniquity weighs down heavily on the sinner and sinks him to the depths of the underworld. If we say that the Almighty helps one bear the weight of his iniquity, it can only be because He shares the burden of responsibility!

In what sense can God share responsibility for sin? If not for God's help, one could not succeed in committing any transgression. If I can prevent an act of sin, but instead stand by and do nothing, then I bear a certain degree of responsibility for the results. Not only does the Almighty not prevent my wrongdoing, but He actually takes an active role in it by giving me the strength to commit the act and sustaining the natural laws that allow such actions to occur. Hence, He bears part of the responsibility for my actions, which in turn relieves me of part of the responsibility.

But doesn't God also take part in the mitzvot I perform? Shouldn't His participation in my mitzvot reduce the merit due me? This is precisely the difference between merit and guilt. If a person sets out to do a good deed and in the process receives help from someone else, the assistance he receives does not diminish from his personal merit. Indeed, the one who lent assistance is awarded credit for the good deed as well. This is not the case, however, with regard to evil. If I received assistance in perpetrating evil without which I could not have succeeded in committing the forbidden act, this diminishes my accountability and the one who could have prevented the act is considered a partner to it. Goodness is positive, and all participants therefore reap the rewards; evil is negative, and the more partners there are, the less personal responsibility each partner bears.

This fact that partnership in good increases the net good whereas partnership in evil diminishes the share of responsibility of each partner may arouse a measure of instinctive agreement, yet it still demands justification. After all, if evil is the other moral side of the coin of free will, why should there be a difference between the responsibility of the partner in virtue, who deserves full credit, and the partner in evil, whose share of blame is proportionate to his share in the action?

The answer to this question is rooted in our understanding of the nature of the balance between good and evil. From the point of view of free will, good and evil are equally balanced, and are therefore equally substantive, but from the point of view of their true metaphysical status, good exists and is real, whereas evil is no more than the absence of existence. One who commits an act of virtue is not only responsible for the beneficial outcome, but has also committed virtue by the very act of choosing, for his choosing reflects the goodness and perfection of God. The act of choosing good is an act of movement towards God, an act of perfection, and as such is itself the embodiment of *kedusha* and the Divine presence in the world. Two people who share in virtue are not only both responsible for the good outcome; each has also created a substantial good in his individual soul and existence, in the world of choice, and each one individually reflects the divine good. The merit is not dependent on the *responsibility for consequences,* but reflects the actual good present in the personality of the free agent of choice, which is independent in each one. The fact that I have partners thus does not diminish the significance of my own choice of the good.

One who chooses evil, on the other hand, does not create anything by his choice, for evil has no inherent substance, and one cannot reflect the existence of negation. His punishment is due to his responsibility for the outcome of his actions, because he is the cause of an evil. Hence, if he has a partner in crime, his responsibility for the outcome is shared, thus limiting his own personal responsibility. Thus, partnership in virtue increases virtue, and partnership in evil divides the evil.

This distinction may explain the principle enunciated by the sages that "a good thought is construed by God as action, and an evil thought is not construed as action" (*Kiddushin* 40a). Concerning good, even if my thoughts and decisions have not been translated into any discernable consequences in the objective world, the very choice and decision to do good serves as the basis for *Shekhina* in the world, for the choice itself is the Divine Presence. This is not true for an evil thought, however, for as long as it has not reached fruition, it has no metaphysical effect and has produced no change in the world of good and evil. Evil does not create, and since there is no consequence, there is no criminal culpability.

It thus emerges that the side of the scale containing my sins – which I chose to commit through my own free will – actually weighs less because God's hand is underneath it. The Almighty takes part of the responsibility for Himself. The side of merits therefore weighs the scales down, even if intrinsically the merits weigh the same as the sins.

Of course, R. Yossi ben Ḥanina's notion stands in opposition to the principle of *beḥira ḥofshit,* which stipulates the human being's full responsibility for what he does. Once we assert God's ability to carry out His will and prevent any action that He opposes, we are no longer truly free to do anything. A person with a strong religious consciousness will not have the free will to murder or refrain from murdering, for example. He will instead calculate that if God wants his enemy to perish, he will perish in any event, and if He does not want his enemy to perish, then he certainly will be unable to kill him. In order to create a world of free will, the Almighty steps back from active involvement – at least overtly – and gives us fixed laws of nature, for the use of which we bear full responsibility, while everything remains in God's power. At the time when one acts, he must not see God's power, for if he does, he has no free will. Afterwards, at the time of judgment, the compassionate, gracious God demonstrates His power and assumes a share of the responsibility for the person's sins. God created the world with free will in order to serve the good, and in the end, He agrees to accept some responsibility for the evil that results from His decision to create the world in this way.

When we recite the Thirteen Attributes, particularly the attribute of *Rav Ḥesed,* we take the closed world that works on the basis of free will and put it into the broader perspective in which the entire world and all natural law lies in God's hands. We bring the Almighty into our world, and, as R. Hutner explained, this infringes upon free will, upon the autonomy of creation. At the time that I call out in the name of *Rav Ḥesed,* I call to God to bear responsibility for the world's substandard condition, to share in the accountability for my wrongful acts. At that moment, the individual foregoes his free will to some extent, returning to that true, primordial point when everything existed solely by His word. And then the scales tilt in favor of kindness.

Chapter Six

Emet

The eighth of the Thirteen Attributes of Mercy is the attribute of *Emet* – "Truth." The inclusion of this quality as a Divine Attribute of Mercy is certainly not intuitive; on the contrary, it would seem that "truth" belongs properly to the realm of strict justice, not mercy. It would seem that the attribute of Truth should dictate that I receive punishment, for this is the *true,* just, and warranted judgment.

It is possible, in fact, to view *Emet* not as a separate attribute, but rather as a description of the previous attribute of *Rav Ḥesed.* According to this approach, instead of reading the phrase, "*Rav Ḥesed veEmet,*" "abundant in kindness and truth," we should read it as "*Rav Ḥesed shel Emet,*" "abundant in truthful kindness." The term "*ḥesed shel Emet*" means perfect kindness, kindness that contains no element at all of possible benefit for the one who dispenses it. Thus, commenting on Jacob's request to Yosef, "you shall do for me truthful kindness" (Genesis 47:29), Rashi explains, "The kindness performed for the deceased is *truthful kindness,* in that one does not anticipate any recompense." Accordingly, there is but a single attribute of *Rav Ḥesed veEmet,* rather than two distinct attributes of *Rav Ḥesed* and *Emet.*

In his Torah commentary, the Ramban explains that *Emet* refers to the kindness that the Almighty performs on behalf of descendants after making a promise to their forebears. Essentially, we deal here with *ḥesed*, but once the *ḥesed* is backed by a divine promise, it becomes *Emet*; the promise lends it a quality of strict law instead of kindness. Justice demands that God fulfill His promise. Accordingly, *Emet* is essentially an attribute of justice rather than kindness, although it reaffirms God's kindness to the patriarchs. Why, then, should *Emet* be counted as a distinct attribute the Thirteen Attributes of Mercy? How does it help preserve the existence of the sinner despite his sin?

In the beginning of *Parashat Va'era*, God tells Moses that although He had revealed Himself to the patriarchs, "I did not make known to them My name of *Havaya*." Rashi explains that God's revelation to the patriarchs was incomplete because "I did not reveal Myself to them through My attribute of Truth, for I promised but did not fulfill." God's promise to give *Eretz Yisrael* to the patriarchs and their descendants was not fulfilled during the patriarchs' lifetimes, and this constitutes a deficiency in the revelation of God's attribute of Truth. God's attribute of Truth is thus the attribute that connects the promise to its fulfillment.

In God's essence, of course, there is no gap at all between His will or promise and their actual fulfillment. The attribute of Truth indicates that the revelation of His will should immediately amount to the fulfillment of it; reality should reflect His will. However, the attribute of Truth is at times concealed; for reasons related to time and how events transpire in this world, promises for the future remain temporarily unfulfilled, as in the case of the promises to the patriarchs.

R. Hutner explains that since Truth is an essential attribute of God, that which is hidden away in the future from our perspective already exists in reality from God's perspective. The concept underlying *Rav Ḥesed*, as we saw, is the "tipping of the scales" in favor of kindness, the notion that goodness always prevails over evil. This ultimate triumph of goodness takes place in the future, as reflected in *Ḥazal*'s comment that *Am Yisrael*'s future repentance is guaranteed. At present, the world is governed by the concept of free will and the balance between good and evil that underlies that principle. But since God is characterized by *Emet*, from His perspective, the future exists already in the present; thus, the attribute of *Rav Ḥesed* can act on behalf of the sinner even now. In other words, the attribute of *Emet* "imports" the decision in favor of goodness from the guaranteed future into the present.

According to this approach, *Emet* is not an independent attribute as much as a part of the attribute of *Rav Ḥesed*; it forms the bridge between the attribute of future repentance and the *Ḥesed* of the present. However, according to Rabbeinu Tam's enumeration of the Thirteen Attributes, we must explain the attribute of *Emet* as an independent attribute, as a separate act of kindness. We are therefore compelled to develop this concept a bit further so that we can gain a clearer understanding.

FREE WILL TO CHOOSE FALSEHOOD

The principle that we are elucidating here is the importance and significance of time. Medieval Jewish philosophy, following the Rambam, accepted the premise that God's existence is above time; time has no meaning for Him. R. Hutner's concept accords with this axiom: God's attribute of *Emet* is the attribute that negates the significance of time as far as He is concerned. From God's perspective, future and present are one and the same. Note that negating the significance of time leads to negating the value of process and progression. Indeed, progress and progression have value only in our world. Truth, on the other hand, is integrally related to timeless eternity; in the Almighty's world, values exist in full in their absolute form – *Emet* – and anything that differs from this absolute truth is called *sheker* (falsehood) and has no right to exist. Therefore – returning to R. Hutner's theory – if God designates something for our future, it must necessarily already exist in His world.

Our world not only includes process and development; the significance of our world is based *entirely* on the value of process. In other words, our world is based upon the precise opposite of the absolute world of God. The added value of the created world is rooted specifically in the value of temporal development. In fact, one can plausibly claim that God created the world in order to achieve the value of process.

This is actually the foundation underlying the concept of free will that we discussed in the previous chapter. Why does God desire *beḥira ḥofshit* (free will) if evil can be chosen as a result? Why is free will a value at all? God could have created man completely good and naturally inclined to choose only goodness, like the angels, without taking the risk that he would choose evil, and without God having to take the responsibility for the evil created by that choice.[1]

The answer is that the true meaning of free will extends beyond the possibility of choosing between two equal possibilities, without being compelled to choose one over the other. If this were the case, *beḥira* would be purely random and bereft of any value and significance. In fact, *Ḥazal* refer to this belief as "*apikorsut*." The Greek philosopher Epicurus, who lent his name to this rabbinic term for heresy, taught that there are random deviations, to the right or to the left, which do not depend on any previous conditions. From *Ḥazal*'s viewpoint, the introduction of a principle of randomness into the world in order to permit freedom constitutes the denial of Providence.[2]

Science, as well as Aristotelian (deterministic) philosophy, is founded upon the notion that every phenomenon results absolutely from the sum of its causes, and there is thus "nothing new under the sun." This scientific thinking has become firmly entrenched within our minds. If I observe a certain phenomenon, I can determine the causes

---

1. The "free will defense" is a common answer to the "problem of evil" – how can evil exist in a world controlled by an omnipotent good God? Free will is itself a good that necessarily implies the possibility of evil (at least the kind of evil that derives from the choices made by free agents). The crucial assumption here is that it is logically impossible to have free will and yet deny the possibility of evil. The English philosopher Anthony Flew asked why God could not create beings possessing free will who, by virtue of their nature, were completely good and therefore always would choose – freely – the good. The question is essentially an extension of the famous discussion regarding what sort of free will is possessed by *tzaddikim*, Kant's "holy personality," whose nature is completely good or who has, after much effort, made himself completely good and virtuous. If one acts virtuously by dint of his inner virtuous nature, does he not have free will? A more radical implication of the discussion concerns the question of whether God, who is wholly good, can be said to have free will. On the one hand, advocates of free will would be undoubtedly reluctant to deny it to God, especially if they were committed to the proposition that all value must be present in God (ethical monotheism). On the other hand, God is the Good, and it is logically necessary that His choices be good. If God's nature does not preclude free will, why can He not create men with the same nature – men who possess free will and a nature that always chooses the good and is repelled by evil?
2. See Rambam, *Guide for the Perplexed* 3:17.

that preceded it; everything preserves its causes in the present and is precisely equivalent to the sum of its causes, no more and no less. If I see a table, then I know that there was a carpenter and wood.

The principle of *beḥira ḥofshit* does not follow this scientific pattern. Through my free will, I can create something that is more than the mechanical development of past causes. The value of *beḥira ḥofshit* lies not only in the ability to choose between two equal possibilities, but also in the ability to create a value that does not exist in the present. In other words, the value of *beḥira* is the value of creativity. God wants the world to exist with *beḥira ḥofshit* because He wants creativity – that goodness be added in places that were less good. Before the world's creation, there was only an absolute value – God – and nothing can be added to an absolute value. There was thus no concept of development, no process of adding something of value, of creating something better in a world that is not absolute goodness. God therefore created an imperfect, faulty, and deficient world in which human beings can use their free will to create goodness where none existed before.

Commenting on the Torah's description of the earth as chaotic, *tohu vavohu* (Genesis 1:2), the midrash writes that from the outset of creation, the Almighty foresaw the conduct of the wicked and the conduct of the righteous (*Bereshit Raba* 2:5). Since the world was, by definition, created imperfect, it must necessarily include the wicked. From amidst this imperfection, *tzaddikim* will also emerge, but not as a natural process like a tree grows from a seed; they will rather emerge as a new creation brought into being through *beḥira ḥofshit*.

TRUTH SHALL GROW FROM THE EARTH

From this viewpoint, our world stands in opposition to divine truth. It is built upon falsehood – the real possibility that goodness will not exist. God created imperfection, which is but a more refined way of saying that He created falsehood. The attribute of Divine Truth cannot help but protest the existence of such a world.

The midrash (*Bereshit Raba* 8:5) writes:

> R. Simon said: At the time when the Almighty came to create man, the ministering angels formed different groups and factions.

> Some said he should not be created, and some said he should be created. This is what is meant when it is written [Psalms 85:11], "Kindness and truth met; justice and peace kissed."

The angels – which, as clearly indicated by the midrash's inference from the verse, refer to the different divine attributes of Kindness, Truth, Justice, and Peace – were divided regarding the value of the human being's creation. Some supported the idea, while others were opposed. "Kindness said he should be created, because he does acts of kindness. But Truth said he should not be created, because he is completely deceitful."

Why did Kindness vote on behalf of man's creation while Truth voted against? Why do we not say that, to the contrary, Kindness objected because man is cruel, and Truth argued in favor because he sometimes speaks the truth? The answer is simple. If a human being sometimes acts kindly and sometimes does not, he may nevertheless be described as a *gomel ḥasadim* (dispenser of kindness). There is value to the kindness he performs, even if he could and should do more. But if a person sometimes speaks truthfully and sometimes lies, then he is "*completely* deceitful." Truth is an absolute value and does not accept any compromises. There is no such thing as a little bit of truth; a little bit of falsehood is equivalent to complete falsehood. Someone who occasionally lies is a liar and can never be trusted. Kindness views the complicated, complex world of the human being as something positive and worthy of existence, whereas Truth sees it as a world of absolute falsehood, something completely negative and bereft of any existential justification.

The midrash advances another example of this struggle between the divine attributes: "Righteousness said that he should be created, because he performs righteousness. Peace said he should not be created, because he is completely contentious." Why is man *completely* contentious? After all, while one may sometimes fight and wage battles, he does live peacefully at other times. But peace, like truth, does not accept compromise. If one lacks total commitment to peace, he is a man of war, a person of strife and contention, even if he sometimes takes a break from the fight. A little bit of war is war and signifies the absolute negation of peace. There is no value to a ceasefire declared by someone who resumes hostilities the next day! A person's righteousness, on the other hand, has value even if he does not continue that mode of behavior consistently.

The Creator's angels cannot agree; should God create man? The midrash skips the argument between righteousness and peace and focuses only on the opposition voiced by the attribute of Truth:

> What did the Almighty do? He took Truth and cast it to the earth. This is what is meant when it is written [Daniel 8:12], "Truth was cast to the earth."

At first glance, the midrash seems to confirm my point. In order to create man, the Almighty must eliminate Truth and demote it from its position of prominence. The world was created as a world of falsehood, a world bereft of Truth.

But can the Almighty act against Truth?

> The ministering angels said before the Holy One, blessed be He: "Master of the worlds! Why do You put to shame Your chief of court?" God replied: "Let Truth rise from the earth!" This is what is meant when it is written [Psalms 85:12], "Truth shall grow from the earth."

The ministering angels advance a compelling argument. The Almighty cannot create man by disgracing the attribute of Truth, the insignia of the King. Truth is not simply an important quality; it is the attribute that includes and forms the basis of every other attribute. An attribute that is not true simply cannot exist. Certainly, nothing can be created on the basis of falsehood!

God responded, "Let Truth rise from the earth." The classic commentaries to *Midrash Raba* explain that the Almighty retracted His decision to cast Truth to the earth and restored it to its place in the heavens; God gave in and accepted the angels' argument. This explanation is untenable, however, as it leaves the question of how man was created given Truth's irrefutable claim that "He should not be created, because he is full of lies.

In my view, we should explain the midrash's conclusion based on the verse it cites at the end of this passage: "Truth shall *grow* from the earth." God does not retract His previous casting of Truth to the earth; Truth remains cast down. God responds to the angels that casting Truth to the earth does not disgrace it, because "Truth shall grow from the earth." The ministering angels thought that Truth must be complete and absolute, existing in the heavens in all its purity without any contact with a deficient, decadent world. God answers that there is another kind of truth, a truth that grows from the earth, from out of falsehood. Indeed, such truth not only does not prevent man's creation, but constitutes the very purpose and goal of man's creation.

The angels, in accordance with the role they so often play in the midrash, express the simple and logical view: falsehood and truth are inherently contradictory. In the mathematics of the angels, something deficient is always worth less than something perfect. God recognizes a much more complex reality, wherein there is a kind of truth that originates from falsehood, or at least from imperfection. In other words, the Almighty seeks the value of process. God created the world in order to achieve the value of progress toward perfection, in addition to the value in that which is perfect and absolute. There is value in the fact that the human being, in his state of imperfection, progressively draws closer to absolute truth. This value has no place in the world of the angels; the realm of objective truth exists there at the highest level, but is static and frozen.

The creation of man, who is "completely deceitful," does not run in opposition to the truth that grows from the earth. To the contrary, the deficient, flawed foundation is necessary for the achievement of this kind of truth. Only the imperfect can form the basis of growth.

The sensitive ear can hear the close association that exists between the attribute of Truth and the attribute that precedes it – *Rav Ḥesed*. In the expression, "*Rav Ḥesed veEmet*," the word "*Rav*" modifies both attributes – *Ḥesed* and *Emet* – and the phrase combines these two attributes together to some extent.[3] Thus, we should refer to the attribute that follows *Rav Ḥesed* not as "*Emet*," but rather as "*Rav Emet*." The attribute of

3. As we mentioned at the outset, this is precisely the reason why some commentators viewed *Rav Ḥesed veEmet* as a single or complex attribute.

"*Rav Emet*" is precisely the midrash's inference from the verse, "Truth shall grow from the earth." *Emet* is an absolute, zealous, and uncompromising attribute. *Rav Emet*, however, is the attribute of Increasing Truth, truth that grows, rises, and emerges, and that from the outset bears relative degrees of more or less. Truth is an attribute of strict justice, but *Rav Emet* is an attribute of *ḥesed*. *Emet* is such a harsh attribute of justice that it not only sentences the sinner to annihilation, it also would prevent the possibility of man's creation in the first place. *Rav Emet*, in contrast, is such a great attribute of *ḥesed* that it not only causes God to tilt the scales of the *beinoni* toward a favorable judgment, it also justifies the existence of the wicked, as it finds value even in the state of evil as the ground from which good can develop in the future.

THE VALUE OF A FLAWED STATE

This analysis leads us to a radical conclusion. Since growth is possible only from a flawed basis, it emerges that the flaw itself has value. Repentance is desirable not merely because it leads to righteousness, but also because growth and progress are intrinsically precious – even more so than the perfect result. Thus, the sin itself has value, as it forms the necessary basis for repentance. The falsehood within man, the condition of deficiency and imperfection, of being corrupted and flawed, is the ground from which truth grows. The angels argue that it is preferable to preserve the unadulterated truth of the heavens, but the Almighty prefers truth that grows from falsehood over pure and absolute truth.

Thus, the divine attributes of kindness include the attribute of *Rav Emet*, an attribute that affords value to heading in the direction of truth. This attribute necessarily assigns merit even to the sin itself and lightens the sinner's judgment, because sin constitutes a necessary component of growth and progression. Of course, this component must be transcended; we do not value sin in order to embrace it, Heaven forbid, but rather so that we can eliminate it. But in the end, when a person's actions are weighed, the scale of guilt becomes lighter, even for the wicked, because their wickedness serves the purpose of truth – on condition that they ultimately repent. The guaranteed eventuality of *teshuva* is the source of the *ḥesed* for the imperfect human being in the present.

R. Hutner understood that the attribute of *Rav Emet* "imports" the value and worth of the future into the present. If a certain present condition leads to a better future, then there is value even in the corrupted present, as it forms the basis for growth. From the perspective of absolute value, we would certainly prefer that the present condition not exist at all, but from the viewpoint of the value of progression and process, there is value in beginning from a state of imperfection in order to reach the point of repentance in the future. The future is thus situated even within the present as the ultimate goal of progress. God is *Rav Emet*; He recognizes the value that can grow from a flawed state more than He values the state of perfection itself.

It is important to stress that without absolute truth, there is no value in developing truth. Process is meaningful only because its aim and destiny is the absolute. The French philosopher Jean-Paul Sartre emphasized the value of movement and development, but because his world did not include existence of God, and hence no possibility of the Absolute, his inevitable conclusion was that movement is the primary component, regardless of the direction taken. In his view, it is important for a person to commit and obligate himself to something, but objectively, the world is essentially absurd. In our worldview, of course, there is good and there is evil, and choosing evil is evil. The value of *beḥira* and of the progression through *teshuva* lies in the fact that the road toward perfection also possesses the value of perfection; *Rav Emet* is *Emet* that grows and rises and aspires to return to its place in the Divine. The value of growth thus lies in the fact that truth makes its way back toward its initial position. In the words of the midrash, the *Emet* that grows from the earth is the same *Emet* that dwelt on high and was cast down, the same attribute that stood before God before man was created.

There is a world of truth; it is found in the future, or in the heavens, in the realm of the ideal, but it certainly exists. There is also a world of *beḥira ḥofshit*, and that world is one of imperfection – "complete deception." The world of free will depends upon the world of truth, and the combination of the two is the truth of God, who created the world of *beḥira* so that it can grow back and reach toward the world of Truth.

There is an important implication of the attribute of *Rav Emet* – God did not create man a *tzaddik*. He created man with free will, which means that He created man imperfect, with the ability to sin. The

Almighty does not desire a naturally righteous person, but rather a person who chooses to be righteous despite the fact that he is not yet righteous. It thus emerges that the not-righteous person – the sinner – is desirable in God's eyes; he is desirable so that he can progress, but he is desirable nonetheless. Ultimately, truth and significance in God's eyes draw part of their essence from deficiency and sin.

There is a custom to recite a prayer called the "Great *Viduy* of Rabbeinu Yona" before *Kol Nidrei* on Yom Kippur eve. This prayer contains one sentence that, if not for the authority of Rabbeinu Yona, would almost appear to be a joke. The worshipper, repenting and begging for compassion, declares, "You should know, HaShem my God, that had I not sinned, I would have been unable to repent." This sounds like a thief who attempts to justify his crime as he returns the goods by saying, "You should know that had I not stolen, I would not have been able to perform the mitzva of returning stolen goods!" Needless to say, Rabbeinu Yona is not recommending that one sin in order to facilitate repentance. Rather, as we have seen, after the fact, we may look upon sin from a certain angle that lends it value. If one indeed repents, then it turns out that even the sin played a positive role.

According to R. Hutner, the attribute of *Emet* is the equation of future and present – the evaluation of the present in light of its future development – for in a world of movement and development, the future is rooted in the present and grants retroactively to the present the value of that which grows out of it. Repentance and future good redeem the present evil, for in the eyes of the merciful God who is *Rav Emet*, the future good is already present in the present evil.

Clearly, the attribute of *Rav Emet* cannot atone for sin; it can only tolerate sin and offer temporary support for the sinner. When the individual is not a *beinoni*, but rather a *rasha* (evil person), when the previous attributes cannot save him and there is nothing in his present condition that has value from the usual point of view, then the perspective that takes the future into account can exonerate him. The previous attributes attempted to justify the person's existence by focusing on the side of him that is good; his merits succeeded in tilting the scale. *Rav Emet* introduces a new, remarkable concept: the side of evil, the side of guilt, can itself serve as a merit. The merits do not outweigh the demerits;

rather, the demerits outweigh themselves. If the sins serve as the basis for improvement, then they, too, may be considered merits. Without the future possibility of change, the *rasha* clearly has no basis for leniency, for it is the eventuality of repentance that is critical in order to justify the ongoing existence of the sinner and the sin.

Chapter Seven

Notzer Ḥesed LaAlafim

The ninth of the Thirteen Attributes of Mercy is *Notzer Ḥesed LaAlafim*, generally translated as, "Preserves Kindness for Thousands [of generations]." In order to understand this attribute, we must explain the precise meaning of all three terms – "*Notzer*," "*Ḥesed*," and "*Alafim*." The meaning of the word "*Notzer*," I believe, holds the key to understanding the phrase "*Ḥesed LaAlafim*," as well.

In his commentary, Rashi explains, "*Notzer Ḥesed* – that which the person performed before Him." According to Rashi, the *ḥesed* described here refers not to the Kindness of the Almighty, but rather the kindness of the human being. When a person performs kindness, God "preserves" it.

The simple and widely accepted interpretation is that this phrase refers to something resembling *zekhut avot*, the merits of our ancestors. In the past, perhaps even in the distant past, people performed kindness, and the Almighty remembers that kindness for thousands of generations on behalf of their descendants. Seforno, for example, comments on this verse, "He keeps (*shomer*) the parents' merit on behalf of the children." If so, *Notzer Ḥesed LaAlafim* parallels the phrase recited toward the beginning of the *Amida* prayer, "*Zokher ḥasdei avot umevi go'el livnei veneihem,*" "He remembers the kindnesses of the fathers, and brings redemption to their descendants."

It seems to me, however, that there is a distinction between *zekhira* ("remembering") and *shemira* ("watching" or "preserving"). *Zekhira* relates to events of the past that no longer exist and are reflected only in one's memory. If I "preserve" something, however, I do not have to remember it, because it is preserved in the present. Thus, *zekhira* relates to the past, whereas *shemira* involves the present.

Moreover, according to this interpretation, why does the verse refer specifically to "*ḥesed*?" If this attribute refers to the virtuous acts of our forefathers, in the merit of which we ask forgiveness, why do we speak only of *ḥesed* and not of their other meritorious deeds? While we often speak of Abraham's piety in particular in terms of his *ḥesed,* the good deeds of the patriarchs certainly include more than generous acts of kindness. I would therefore suggest that the term *Notzer Ḥesed* means something other than "*Zokher Ḥesed.*"

THE JUSTICE OF *ZEKHUT AVOT*

Most importantly, there is an essential difference between the principle of *zekhut avot* and the attribute of *Notzer Ḥesed LaAlafim* that appears in the context of the Thirteen Attributes. Whereas *Notzer Ḥesed* is an attribute of mercy, *zekhut avot* is a reflection of justice.

We intuitively sense a certain logic and measure of justice in the idea of *zekhut avot,* the concept that children are rewarded or punished on account of their forefathers' conduct. Consider the case of a person to whom I am grateful, but who passes away before I could properly reward him. It would make sense to pay him for his deeds by assisting his children; we remember the "*ḥesed avot*" and favor the children in their father's merit. At the same time, we are uncomfortable with this notion; why does someone deserve to be favored simply because he has a meritorious father? The Gemara (*Berakhot* 7a) resolves this problem by adding a condition – the children must follow their parents' mode of conduct in order to receive their parents' reward.

The concept of *zekhut avot* is the converse of the notion of "*poked avon avot*" – that God brings punishment for the parents' wrongdoing upon their descendants. This appears, at first glance, to contradict the admonition, "Fathers shall not die on account of sons, and sons shall not die on account of their fathers" (Deut. 24:16). Corresponding to its interpretation of *zekhut avot,* the Gemara explains that "*poked avon avot*" applies when the children continue their parents' sinful behavior. This notion is grounded in the logic of strict justice, and the converse situation of merit and reward possesses a similar logic: one who follows his parents' model of virtue benefits from their merit, but not if he turns his back on his parents' way of life.[1] This does not refer to a son who is righteous exactly like his father, but rather one who "continues" the father's way; the guidance he received from his father continues to steer him, even if he stumbles on one occasion or another. The attribute of Justice agrees that a child who follows his parents' virtuous ways should reap some of the benefits of their merits.

In contrast, "*Notzer Ḥesed LaAlafim*" does not reflect justice, but mercy. This attribute has no limit, but rather extends for "thousands" of generations. This clearly indicates that it is not rooted in justice, for justice, by definition, is limited to the just and proper degree of reward. The principle of *zekhut avot,* which operates through the system of justice, therefore has a limit based upon the amount of merit the parents amassed.

The limits of *zekhut avot* are indicated by the Gemara (*Shabbat* 55a), which cites the statement of Shmuel, "*Zekhut avot* is finished." The Gemara suggests several different possibilities regarding when *zekhut avot* was exhausted, all of them during the First Temple period. One suggestion is that it ended during the time of Ḥaza'el king of Aram, about which it is written, "God was gracious unto them, and had mercy on them, and He turned to them for the sake of His covenant with Abraham, Isaac, and Jacob, and He did not wish to destroy them, and

1. Whereas a positive benefit may result from the attribute of Justice, if it is deserved, or from *Ḥesed,* if it is pure grace and mercy, suffering can only be due to the attribute of Justice; in theory, there should be no concept of undeserved suffering. (If not for this assumption, the "problem of evil" would not exist.) There is no divine attribute of cruelty. Hence, we have a test mechanism to determine whether a given benefit derives from Justice or Mercy: if a certain good has a parallel evil, if a benefit has a parallel suffering, then since the latter must necessarily belong to the realm of justice, the good does as well. It follows that *zekhut avot,* as a parallel to *poked avon avot,* belongs to the attribute of Justice, and not to Mercy.

He did not cast them from His presence *as yet*" (II Kings 13:23). Rashi explains, "'As yet' – but from then on He *did* cast them away, and He paid no attention to the covenant of the fathers." The Gemara goes on to bring the opinion of R. Yehoshua b. Levi, who dates the end of *zekhut avot* to the time of Elijah, earlier than the reign of Ḥaza'el. In that case, on what did God base His remembering of the covenant at the time of Ḥaza'el? Rashi explains, "It was through the operation of mercy [alone] that [the covenant] was remembered for them in the time of Ḥaza'el." In other words, *zekhut avot* is not mercy, but *din*, which is why is can be exhausted; however, even when the limit is reached, the attribute of mercy continues. *Zekhut avot* has a limit, but the attribute of mercy and graciousness has none.

Tosafot cites a different opinion in the name of Rabbeinu Tam, who asks why we continue to mention *zekhut avot* in our prayers if it has already been exhausted. His answer is that even though *zekhut avot* has ended, "*brit avot*" has not; our prayers are based on *brit*, covenant, and not on *zekhut*, merit. God committed Himself to a covenant, including an obligation not to abandon the Jewish People, and this promise obligates God irrespective of the actions or merit of the fathers. God fulfills His covenant even if His continued providence is unmerited on the basis of the deeds of the fathers and the children. This is a kind of *din* – not one of reward and punishment, but rather of obligation. God's promises must be kept.

In any event, there is a clear essential distinction between *zekhut avot*, which is based on the principle of justice and which can therefore be exhausted, and the attribute of *Ḥesed*, about which it is written:

> For the mountains shall move, and the hills shall fall, but My *Ḥesed* shall not be moved from you, and the covenant of My peace shall not fall, says HaShem who has mercy on you (Isaiah 54:10).

In our context of the Thirteen Attributes of Mercy, the attribute of Justice objects, and demands punishment. By the time the sinner has arrived at the ninth Attribute of Mercy, the power of God's attributes of Kindness and Compassion have been insufficient to save him. *Notzer Ḥesed LaAlafim* must thus indicate something other than remembering *zekhut avot*, which reflects the justice of paying a child the debt owed to his parents. We must therefore explain that this attribute gives the child more than he or his parents deserve.

THE PRESERVER OF *ḤESED* THROUGH ETERNITY

A good deed warrants reward, and this obligation is sustained through memory: "All your deeds are inscribed in the book, and the Employer can be trusted to pay your reward." The repercussions of a good deed, however, extend beyond the reward. A good deed is inherently good; it entails the creation of a situation of goodness, value and sanctity, and increases the *Shekhina*'s manifestation in the world. What happens to that goodness, to the metaphysical reality of value and worth, after the deed is completed? Where does it go?

The *Rishonim* emphasized that the reward in the next world is not truly a reward or repayment, but rather an acquired reality. A good person earns a spiritual existence according to his attainments in this world, whether in terms of intellect (Rambam), his love of God (R. Hasdai Crescas), or spiritual attachment (R. Yehuda HaLevi). A person's actions leave an imprint upon his soul and character; we are all the product of our actions and experiences. But this result of goodness expires once a person dies; the positive impact of goodness on the soul certainly cannot be transferred to someone else – not even to one's child who follows his ways.

Furthermore, if we consider that the value of life lies not in the results of one's progress, but in the progress itself, in the ascending towards God, as we explained in the previous attribute, what happens to that goodness, that reflection of God's perfection, once the deed is done and accomplished? The value of an act lies in the movement, in the ascent, the process of improvement and drawing closer to perfection. Since the divine image and the chariot of the *Shekhina* are sustained through the person's ascent towards perfection, the moment he stops moving, nothing remains of the value of movement, even if he rests on a high level. There is a famous story attributed to the Ba'al Shem Tov that concludes with the sentence, "All of life in the World to Come is going from strength to strength and from level to level, from now and forever." One who stops is like a corpse, a stone.

Remembering suffices to obligate payment for a good deed, but it cannot preserve the actual worth of the good deed, the value of the progress towards God. If I give charity to a poor person, the "Employer" can be trusted to pay me my due reward, even many years later; the merit assuredly remains. But what remains of the goodness itself even a year after the act? The money is already gone, and the poor man himself may no longer be alive. What is left from that kindness?

The words of a French poet reverberate: "*Où sont les neiges d'antan*?" Where are the snows of yesteryear? Youngsters do not generally look back longingly at lost time, but rather continue to flow onward. It is only at a certain age that we begin to sense the loss of time, wondering, "Where are those precious moments?" Psychologists might classify this feeling as nothing more than nostalgia, but metaphysically, this is a real question. What happens to the goodness that a person creates, if it all depends on time – and time passes?

The Ibn Ezra is reputed to have expressed the fragility of time succinctly in a famous passage: "The past is gone, the future is not yet, and the present is like the blink of an eye." The past is gone; it no longer exists. Does the goodness, the sanctity that we have created, similarly disappear and leave behind only a memory? Where is that moment a year ago on Yom Kippur, when I rose to higher levels of closeness with God? Is the memory of that moment all that remains?

The answer to this question is *Notzer Ḥesed LaAlafim*. God keeps and preserves kindness for thousands of generations; He maintains it in a reality beyond the reality of ephemeral progress, which every year passes away. Note Rashi's formulation in the comment cited earlier: "*Notzer Ḥesed* – that which the person performed *before Him*." The kindness a person performed is offered to God like a sacrifice; it is presented "before Him," and God therefore preserves it in His own reality, which is eternal and beyond time. The goodness we create in the world is time-dependent, but in God's reality, past, present, and future combine – "*HaShem Melekh, HaShem Malakh, HaShem Yimlokh LeOlam VaEd*" ("The Lord reigns, the Lord has reigned, the Lord shall reign for all eternity!").

The same values that we exhibit in this world, the reflection of divine perfection, exist absolutely and supra-temporally within the divine reality. As we explained in the previous chapter, our *Emet*, the truth that grows and develops, is the same as the absolute Truth that constitutes the "insignia of the Almighty." Our truth reflects divine Truth in a partial and deficient manner, and that divine Truth sustains the growth of our truth – "Truth shall grow from the earth." Similarly, the good that we perform is significant because it is, indeed, true goodness, divine goodness, and is identical to the *Shekhina*'s presence in the world. A good deed disappears upon the completion of that deed, but if I created a reality of *Shekhina* in the world, it still exists in God's timeless reality.

The concept that God preserves our *ḥesed* in His timeless reality is implicit in the Ramban's interpretations of the word "*Notzer*." He first defines this word as synonymous with "*Shomer*" (to "keep" or "preserve"), and then suggests a second meaning – that it means "Growth," as in the phrase, "*venetzer misharashav yifreh*," "and a *sprout* shall blossom from its roots" (Isaiah 11:1). God, according to this second approach, makes *ḥesed* "grow" for thousands of generations.

This approach does not contradict the first, but rather explains it – God preserves *ḥesed* by making it grow. The *ḥesed* that a person performs is itself a living entity whose life force is the movement that I made, my rising from one level to another. The actual result of my actions has no worth from the perspective of the supreme value – it is certainly worth less than the perfect, absolute, and eternal value – but God values the movement itself, the ascent, making that which is deficient less deficient. The moment one has stopped moving forward, and certainly after one has died, nothing should remain. The performance of a mitzva is like the planting of a seed. If I stop watering it, if I stop ascending further, then only a memory will remain of the seed that I planted; it either grows or dies.

But in God's mercy, this is not what happens. God is *Notzer Ḥesed* – He makes my *ḥesed* grow for thousands of generations. God looks upon us from a dynamic, process-oriented perspective, so that I equal more than what I am in the present. God, who exists beyond time, views me not as a static creature, but rather as a complete stream of past leading to the future, and my value is thus infinite. From the perspective of *Notzer Ḥesed LaAlafim*, I have the value of *kedusha* and *Shekhina*; I am a human reflection of Perfection.

The two interpretations offered by the Ramban are essentially one and the same. What makes our *ḥesed* grow? The *shemira* – the fact that God "preserves" it. The linkage of the past to the present and the future to form a single process gives eternal life to man's actions.

If I, a tiny midget, can stand on the shoulders of a giant and manage to progress one millimeter, then I continue the process, and my value thus equals that of the entire process. The millimeter itself is not worth much, but the progress is worth eternity, because it is preserved in God's reality. I have created something that had not yet existed in the world. A tree that lives and grows has immense value, even if at the moment it is a tiny sapling.

The *ḥesed* of man takes part in the establishment of the *Shekhina* in the world, and in so doing, it joins the eternity of God. Hence, the continuation by the children of the edifice of *ḥesed* established by the fathers is part of the continued eternal existence of the Divine Presence. If the children were to be exterminated, God forbid, there would be nothing left of the Divine Presence in the world. It is thus not the memory of God that preserves this *ḥesed* of the fathers, but His *Shekhina,* which is perpetuated through the existence of the children. The mercy of God preserves the children who continue in the path of the fathers – the present continuation of the past – for He is *Notzer Ḥesed LaAlafim.*

The Preserver of *Ḥesed* Through Eternity preserves the past and connects it with the future. We speak not of the merit of the past, but rather of the merit that exists in the present as a result of the present person being part of a living, developing process. The entire process is viewed as a single, all-inclusive present. Therefore, even if there is a perfect balance between one's merits and demerits, from the perspective of *Notzer Ḥesed,* they are not equal at all, because this attribute views the merits as part of an infinite framework of progress toward perfection.

THE VALUE OF PROGRESS

Now that we have explained the meaning of the term *Notzer,* let us proceed to the other words in this phrase.

Rashi explains "*Alafim*" to mean "two thousand." The explanation of the *Midrash HaGadol,* however, appears closer to the straightforward meaning of the verse: "It does not say, 'For a thousand generations,' but rather, 'for thousands' – for thousands of thousands of generations."[2] In Biblical Hebrew, infinity is described by a large number, beyond what people can normally perceive; "*Alafim*" thus refers to an infinite period of time.

This attribute does not describe mere multiplication of *ḥesed*, but rather a fundamentally different kind of calculation. A *ḥesed* in the present can be assigned a certain weight in quantitative terms, but the preservation and "growth" of the *ḥesed* gives it inestimable value – the value of moving closer to perfection. That which increases infinitely is equivalent to the infinite, the value of the *Shekhina*. From this perspective, God does not simply tilt the scales in favor of the side of merit, but rather decides definitively that the merits are worth "thousands of thousands."

This also explains, I believe, why the verse chooses specifically the term "*ḥesed*," which expresses giving to others. *Ḥesed* entails adding on to something of value. The *Shekhina*'s presence in the world is based upon the *ḥesed* we and our forefathers perform, as it were, for the *Shekhina*. These kindnesses are the stem that continues to grow as a result of God's preservation and nurturing.

The value of progress is not merely the value of my life as an individual, but rather my value as part of the history of *Am Yisrael*, the value of the life of a nation. The movement that began during the lives of the patriarchs has not yet ended. Even if the process is temporarily at rest, and even if the process sometimes regresses in the lives of individuals, from the broader perspective encompassing the lives of the patriarchs to this very day and beyond, the overall direction is one of progress and growth, toward *Shekhina* and perfection. So long as I remain part of this process and have not abandoned it – as long as my life is devoted to continually drawing close to the Almighty and sanctifying His name in the world – yesterday's kindness still exists today and still retains its value.

Abraham never rested – he travelled, journeyed, and "walked

2. This is, indeed, stated explicitly by Rashi in his comments to *Makkot* 23a, where he explains that according to the simple reading of the verse, *LaAlafim* refers to the end of all the generations, as opposed to *Ḥazal*'s midrashic reading, which interprets it to mean two thousand.

before God in order to be perfect."[3] His movement continues through his descendants and disciples – not the actions he performed, but rather the path he chose,[4] the "*Lekh Lekha*" command he received which defined the rest of his life, as well as our own.

When we recite "*Notzer Ḥesed LaAlafim*," we must understand and commit ourselves to join the generational chain, to sense that we continue the project begun by our patriarchs. We are not trying to use our "connections," but rather to invoke our continuation of their path. This means not simply preserving the values of our patriarchs, but advancing them, continuing the forward movement and progress. One who appeals to the attribute of *Notzer Ḥesed LaAlafim* claims to be not a fixed good reality, but rather a reality that may be bad, but which improves. This improvement has value as part of the great progression that encompasses all of human history.

3. See Genesis 12:3, 12:9, 13:17, 17:1.
4. "For I know him, that he will command his children and his household after him, and they will keep the path of God, to do righteousness and justice" (ibid. 18:19).

Chapter Eight

Noseh Avon VaFesha VeḤata'a

In this chapter, we will discuss three different Attributes that the Torah combines with the shared verb of "*noseh*" – "*Noseh Avon VaFesha VeḤata'a*" – "forgives iniquity, transgression, and sin."[1]

Although the words *avon, pesha,* and *ḥata'a* may have different connotations, all three mean "sin." One could thus argue that this phrase should in fact be counted as but a single attribute; the act of *noseh* refers to only one act of kindness. *Ḥazal,* however, conveyed a tradition that these verses express Thirteen Attributes of Mercy, thus compelling us to view this phrase as listing three distinct attributes and to explain them as such. The Ramban similarly notes in his Torah commentary:

Since the act of forgiveness is not equivalent in the cases of

1. This translation of the three Hebrew terms for sin is rather arbitrary. In the course of the chapter, we will explain the precise meaning of each term, but for the purposes of translation we will assume that *avon* = iniquity; *pesha* = transgression; and *ḥata'a* = sin.

> iniquity, transgression, and sin, but rather each features a special aspect, each one is called an independent attribute.

We must therefore explain the "special aspect" within each of these three instances of forgiveness.

THREE TYPES OF SIN

Ḥazal explain the precise meanings of *avon, pesha,* and *ḥata'a* in the context of their discussion of the proper sequence in which they should be listed in the *Kohen Gadol*'s confession on Yom Kippur (*Yoma* 35b).[2] The Mishna records the text as, "*Aviti, pashati, ḥatati lefanekha*" ("I have acted iniquitously, transgressed, and sinned before You"). The Gemara attributes this view to R. Meir and cites a *Beraita* that points to two instances in the Torah where this sequence appears. In describing the *Kohen Gadol*'s confessional before dispatching the *se'ir hamishtale'aḥ* ("scapegoat"), the Torah writes, "And he shall confess over it all the iniquities of the Israelites, and all their transgressions including all their sins" (Leviticus 16:21). The verse containing the Thirteen Attributes similarly records the terms in this order – "*Noseh Avon VaFesha VeḤata'a.*" The *Ḥakhamim,* however, have a different opinion:

> The *Ḥakhamim* say: *Avonot* – these are intentional violations, as is written, "That soul shall be utterly cut off; its *avon* is upon it."
>
> *Pesha'im* – these are rebellions, as it is written, "The king of Moab *pasha* against me."
>
> For all their *Ḥata'ot* – these are unintentional sins, as is written, "A soul that shall sin (*teḥeta*) unintentionally."
>
> Now, once he has confessed the intentional sins and the rebellions, does he again confess unintentional sins?! Rather, thus should he confess: "*ḥatati, aviti, pashati lefanekha.*" And so is writ-

2. It should be noted that the sages afforded great importance to proper sequence. The Gemara establishes rules regarding the sequence in which to perform multiple actions required at the same time (such as "*tadir veshe'eino tadir, tadir kodem*"), as well as the sequence of reciting *berakhot* and prayers (such as the *berakhot* in the *Amida* service).

> ten by David, "*ḥatanu* with our fathers, *he'evinu, reshanu.*" And so by Daniel, "*ḥatanu, ve'avinu, veḥartanu, umaradnu.*"

The majority view of the *Ḥakhamim* maintains that the *Kohen Gadol* confessed in the sequence of "*ḥatati aviti ufashati,*" moving progressively from the less severe type of sin to the most severe: unintentional violations (*ḥatati*), intentional violations (*aviti*), and then acts of rebellion (*pashati*).

Although the *Ḥakhamim* cite proofs of their own for this sequence, they must explain the sequence of the phrase in the Thirteen Attributes, from which R. Meir drew proof for his position, and in which *ḥata'a* is listed last. The *Ḥakhamim* explain:

> Moses said before the Almighty: Master of the world! When Israel sin before You and repent, transform their willful violations into unintentional violations.

Rashi explains, "This is what [the verse] says: He forgives *avon* and *pesha* as a *ḥatat* – an unintentional violation." In order to justify the illogical sequence in this verse, the *Ḥakhamim* introduce an alternate reading and an entirely new concept; *ḥata'a* is not a third subject of the verb "*noseh,*" but rather the goal of the forgiveness of the other two types of sin. In offering His forgiveness, God turns willful violations (*avon*), and even more severe acts of betrayal (*pesha*), into *ḥata'a,* unintentional violations.

The *Ḥakhamim's* reading of our verse leaves us with a number of questions. First, according to their interpretation, the phrase "*Noseh Avon VaFesha VeḤata'a*" contains only two attributes: *Noseh Avon* – God forgives *avonot* by treating them as unintentional violations – and *Noseh Pesha* – God forgives *pesha'im* by treating them as unintentional violations. The enumeration of the Thirteen Attributes requires that we consider *Noseh Avon VaFesha VeḤata'a* as three Attributes, and not just two. Moreover, this reading is clearly not the plain meaning of the verse, according to which the verb *noseh* refers to three objects – *avon, pesha,* and *ḥata'a.*

On a more basic level, what does it mean that the Almighty forgives sins as though they were committed unintentionally? This question is both a philosophical and a moral problem. Philosophically, how does a willful violation change into an inadvertent sin? And from the perspective of morality, what is the point of such a transformation? After all, inadvertent sins also require atonement; the entire institution of *korban ḥatat* (sin offering) in the Temple applies to cases of unintentional sin. Why does God treat willful violations as *shegagot,* reducing the severity of punishment without forgiving completely?

The Gemara concludes by ruling in accordance with the *Ḥakhamim* sequence, but the difficulty with their approach is duly noted:

> Raba bar Shmuel said in the name of Rav: The halakha follows the view of the *Ḥakhamim.*
>
> Is this not obvious? When the minority opposes the majority, halakha follows the majority! One might have contended that R. Meir's reasoning is more plausible, since the verse regarding Moses [in the context of the Thirteen Attributes] supports him. Hence, we are taught [that the halakha nevertheless follows the view of the *Ḥakhamim*].

Even after the *Ḥakhamim* suggested their amended reading of the Attributes, the Gemara views this verse as a compelling reason to consider accepting R. Meir's view:

> A certain person went down [to lead the prayer service] in the presence of Raba, and acted in accordance with R. Meir. He [Raba] said to him: You reject the *Ḥakhamim*'s view and act in accordance with R. Meir? He said to him: I hold like R. Meir, as is written in the Torah of Moses.

Clearly, the Talmudic sages did not readily accept the new interpretation of *Noseh Avon VaFesha VeḤata'a,* even many years after the halakha was decided according to *Ḥakhamim.*

DILUTING THE EFFECT OF SIN

In order to understand the meaning of the verse according to the *Ḥakhamim* and to understand these three attributes, we must first explain the concept of "*Noseh Avon.*" What is the meaning of this attribute in the context of the nine previous attributes? I contend that this phrase marks a transition within the Thirteen Attributes and brings us into an entirely different realm than the one in which the previous attributes operate.

Until now, as we have emphasized on several occasions, the purpose of the Attributes of Mercy was to sustain the individual, to grant the sinner the possibility of existing despite his sin and annul, or at least mitigate, his punishment. Although sin affects the person's connection and relationship to God, the God of Mercy has the power to overcome the damage to the relationship and continue sustaining the individual. In the context of the first nine attributes, the discussion revolved around the person – his life, his existence, and his ability to stand before God. Now, however, the focus has moved from the person – the one who committed the sin – to the sin itself.

According to *Ḥazal*, a sin does not merely anger God; it is inherently negative. Even if God did not care about the sin, it should still concern the person himself, because the existence of sin in his life and in his personality is harmful, contaminating, and destructive. Throughout the writings of the prophets, sin is described as filth, a stain, dirt, and mud. The Ramban speaks of how a sin "dulls" the soul. This effect of sin does not depend upon a person's account with God; even if God consents not to punish us for our sins, they still damage our souls and our world.

It is at this point that the three attributes of *Noseh Avon VaFesha VeḤata'a* come into play. After the successful effects of the previous attributes, we turn to the Almighty and declare, "It is good that I exist, but my spiritual health is at risk." We need God's kindness to immunize us, to prevent the harmful effects of the sin from destroying our lives. In the previous attributes, the sinner's only interest is survival; he does not address reparation. It is only at this point that the process of *teshuva* has at last begun to unfold. Thus, the Gemara places in Moses' mouth the words, "When Israel sin before You and repent…" In calling upon these Attributes, we ask God to neutralize the harmful impact of our sin by transforming them into *shegagot*, unintentional sins.

The verse distinguishes between three different types of adverse effects caused by sin, corresponding to the three different types of sin – *avon*, *pesha*, and *ḥata'a*. The difference between them lies not only in the level of their severity, a quantitative difference, but rather the type of impact they have upon the individual, a qualitative difference. Indeed, if the difference lay only in a relative degree of severity, forgiveness would be one and the same for all three kinds of sins, and we would have here only one attribute, not three. The Ramban comments, however, that the manner of forgiveness differs with regard to an *avon*, *pesha*, and *ḥata'a*; the Almighty "immunizes" against the effects of each category in a different way.

In the context of confession, the sequence of the terms is logically determined based on the severity of the sin described. I request for atonement based on the gravity of the act committed, from lightest to most severe. In the context of the Thirteen Attributes, however, we do not speak of confession, nor of a request for forgiveness, but rather of a request for protection against the harmful effects of sin. Here, it is not the gradation of severity that determines the sequence, but rather the kind of harm caused, the kind of "poison" that the sin injects into a person's reality.

Three different injuries result from sin:

***AVONOT*:**

What is damaged by an intentional sin? An intentional sin is evil, and hence it damages the Good. The world, both the world as a whole and the person's internal world, is the handiwork of the Almighty and embodies the divine good. Sin is evil; it is a reality of evil, and its existence damages the divine goodness. Evil and sin damage and ruin goodness itself. The world is less good than it was, and even the person himself, as a complete world of his own, is less good. An existence that is not good is a deficient existence.

Ḥazal explain that even the physical order of the world is negatively affected by sin. They claim, for example, that the destruction of the Temple had an adverse effect upon the flavor of fruits, and that the sins of the generation of the Flood harmed the world's natural order ("*Vatishaḥet ha'aretz*," "The earth was corrupted;" Genesis 6:11). If even the natural order is affected by the presence of evil, then certainly the spiritual order, the spiritual well-being of the world and the individual, is harmed by *avon*.

PESHA'IM:

Rebellion, by definition, entails opposing someone or his authority, as demonstrated by the verse cited in the Gemara, "the king of Moab *pasha* against me." While *avonot* adversely affect the divine good, *pesha'im* adversely affect divine kingship. One who intentionally commits a sin – and certainly one who sins inadvertently – does not infringe upon God's kingship, because he had no intention to rebel against divine authority. His intent was not to oppose the rule of the King of the world. But some people go farther, transgressing in order to rebel, to protest God's rule. Every *pesha* also includes an *avon* – but not every *avon* includes a *pesha*.

ḤATA'A:

Shegagot are not evil by nature, because the transgressor had no intention to do evil, and certainly not to rebel. The act may be the same, but there is clearly a difference, for in the absence of evil intent, no harm is caused to God's goodness or His kingship.

Obviously, we would prefer that God forgive our sins altogether, but this is not up for discussion at the moment. At this point, the sinner is not trying to save himself, but rather to prevent the harmful effects of his sin. He therefore asks God to make his sins like *shegagot*, thereby preventing the metaphysical impact of his wrongdoing.

BEARING SIN

How does this happen? How does the Almighty protect and preserve His goodness and kingship from the effects of sin? He is *Noseh Avon VaFesha VeḤata'a*." "*Noseh*" literally means to "bear" or "carry." When someone bears my burden, he lightens the crushing weight by taking it upon himself. Our sins "affect" the Almighty by damaging divine goodness and kingship, but from the Almighty's perspective, my sins cannot truly have an adverse effect, for God is boundless good and asserts absolute, unlimited kingship. True, as we discussed in our first installment in this series, if we accept God's kingship, then He is king, and if not, then He is not a king. However, the opposite is also true. In our world, Divine kingship depends on us. However, in the world of the transcendent, absolute God, who was, is and will always be, His kingship and goodness are absolute and not dependent on any factor whatsoever. "Master of the world, who reigned before any creature was created" precedes ", at the time when all by His will is done, then His name is called, 'King.'" If the Almighty takes the "damage" and evaluates it from His absolute perspective, then there is no damage at all. In the world of creation, every misdeed harms the *Shekhina,* but in the upper world, there is nothing man can do that could infringe one iota upon Divine Perfection. By bearing the weight of sins, God lets them be absorbed into His infinite goodness and infinite kingship, and the damage is diluted beyond existence.

In the Rosh HaShana liturgy, we recite two *berakhot* related to the theme of *malkhut* (divine kingship). The second, which we call "*Malkhuyot,*" begins with the passage:

> We therefore hope for You, the Lord our God, to soon behold the glory of Your might... to perfect the world through the kingship of *Sha-dai,* whereupon all human beings shall call on Your name.

This kingship is one of human acceptance, of coronation. Therefore, at that time, "the Lord shall be King over the entire earth" and "on that day (and only on that day) the Lord shall be one, and His name one." Before this *berakha,* however, we recite a different *berakha* of kingship, one that is embedded within the *berakha* of *kedushat HaShem* (*HaMelekh HaKadosh*):

> And so, instill Your fear, O Lord our God, within all Your creations... and all evil, in its entirety, will disappear like smoke.

If God appears in all His glory and all His fearful might, then evil, which now appears to be a major defect in His kingship, would turn out to be no more than a whiff of smoke – dispersed in the wind, and then nothing at all. We can accept God's rule, but He can also force His rule upon His subjects, and at that point, evil turns out to be nothing – it "disappears like smoke."

As we explained in our discussion of *Rav Ḥesed,* such an action would undermine the value of free will and human initiative, but for the same reason, and to the same extent, it eliminates the negative quality of evil. Sin can cause harm to the immanent *Shekhina*, but God, in His kindness, can rise above everything to the transcendent level, where nothing can be diminished. The Almighty takes the *avonot* and *pesha'im* upon Himself. He "bears *avon*" – and goodness cannot truly be harmed; He "bears *pesha*" – and His kingship cannot be undermined to even the slightest extent.

PROTECTING THE SOUL FROM SIN

Although *ḥata'a*, unintentional sin, does not damage God's goodness or His kingship, it has a negative impact nonetheless. The Ramban has a clearly defined theory regarding the concept of *shegaga*, which is rooted in his general approach to theological anthropology. According to the Ramban, *shegaga* implies an act committed without any guilt on the person's part. Nevertheless, despite the absence of evil or guilt, the sin itself necessitates atonement, because sin is inherently poisonous for the soul. One who unintentionally swallows poison is no less at risk than one who does so willfully. In the language of the Ramban:

> For every forbidden thing sullies the soul and defiles it … and that is why the unintentional transgressor is called a sinner. Nevertheless, the unintentional transgressor does not deserve a punishment for his transgression in *Gehinom* and the pit of iniquity, but he requires cleansing from that sin, and he must purify and sanctify himself so that he be worthy of the proper station for his good deeds in the World to Come.[3]

In his discussion of the question of *tzaddik ve'ra lo*, the suffering of the righteous, the Ramban similarly proposes (as one of his suggestions) that the suffering *tzaddik* committed transgressions unintentionally. Being guiltless, he is still defined as a *tzaddik*, but the sin nevertheless adheres to his soul and injures it. The inadvertent sinner needs not to be punished, but to be healed; an operation is necessary to clean out the sin from the recesses of the soul – and at times, this procedure entails pain.

Just as willful violations have a harmful effect on goodness and

3. *Torat HaAdam*, in *Kitvei HaRamban* (Mossad HaRav Kook), vol. 2, p. 270.

acts of rebellion affect divine kingship, unintentional sins affect a person's soul, the reflection of sanctity within him. *Shegagot* ruin the divine image within a person. The soul of a sinner is a soul that has taken ill. God, in His kindness, may disregard the sin, and it may not have a negative effect on the world because it was committed accidentally, but the person nevertheless suffers from the very presence of sin within his character, from the destructive influence that sin wields upon the soul.

We explained that God can absorb the damage to goodness and kingship within His absolute, infinite goodness and kindness, but how does the attribute of *Noseh Ḥata'a* work? With regard to *avon* and *pesha*, the solution is to consider them unintentional sins, thereby neutralizing the harm. In the case of a *shegaga*, however, the harm does not depend on intent, and rather results from the inherent negative quality of the act itself. How can God protect the soul?

The answer is essentially the same. Only the Almighty Himself, who is perfect and absolute, can absorb the blow without enduring any effect. One can harm divine kingship in the world, but if the Almighty joins His kingship in the world to His kingship in the heavens, no harm can be done. The same applies to the human being. The sanctity of the soul can be ruined, but if the Almighty joins the person's soul with the Divine Soul above, if He once again blows a fresh soul of life in man's nostrils, then man will be renewed as a new living creature. The soul itself will retain its purity, unharmed and unaffected by the sin.

Of course, there is a fundamental Jewish precept not to confuse Creator and creature. I am not part of God, but rather the image of God. We previously spoke of the fact that God identifies with the divine image, and this forms the basis of the attribute of *Ḥanina*. Here, we speak of a more extreme form of identity – not an attribute based on merely psychological identification, not the arousal of feeling and participation in pain as a result of that identification, but rather a degree of identity, or, more accurately, a degree of continuity. God, through his identification and connection with the pure soul that He breathed into man,[4] changes the context from the lone individual collapsing under the burden of his

4. Commenting on the verse, "He breathed a living soul into his nostrils" (Genesis 2:7), the Ramban writes, "One who breathes, from within himself he breathes."

sins to a person whose soul is bound at its root with the Divine Throne of Glory – so that, at least at his core, he is part of an infinite, absolute, and perfect system. This act of divine kindness allows for the possibility of purifying anew the damaged soul, curing it and healing it of its illness.

Man, due to his potential, is bound to the transcendent sanctity above, and hence is immune to the harmful effects of sin. The extent of God's attachment of His supreme existence to our existence can serve as a source for purifying the entire personality. As we have stressed before, "Had the verse not been written, it would have been impossible to say."

Here, too, we encounter a contradiction of sorts between this divine attribute of kindness and the precept of *beḥira ḥofshit* at the foundation of the world's creation. The world was not created to be connected with the immune, infinite world of the Creator. To the contrary, we were created to be independent, capable of making decisions autonomously, with the ability to pollute and ruin, to destroy and to detract from the world – but in the hope that we instead will choose to build and purify, to improve and become holy. *Noseh Ḥata'a* is the response to an illness, and it signifies a retreat from the purpose of creation. If a man is immunized from the consequences of his actions, he loses responsibility for his actions, and it follows that he loses the significance of his free will. Nevertheless, in order to be able to choose and become holy tomorrow, one must be purified today.

If God allows creation to operate only according to the rules of free choice and independence, it will become so polluted that no progress will be possible; the cancer of sin will ultimate kill the patient. It is therefore necessary for the attribute of *Ḥesed* to get involved, and this involvement is based upon the truth that the human soul is a part of God from above: "Heal me, O Lord, and I shall be healed; save me, and I shall be saved – for *You* are *my* glory" (Jeremiah 17:14). The glory of man, which heals him, is God.

God does not allow goodness to be corrupted, divine kingship to be humbled, or the soul from God above to be polluted. God transforms the intentional sin and the act of rebellion into a *shogeg*, and even the *shogeg* – the inherent, negative impact of every sin – He eliminates. This final stage is not expressed in the Gemara's discussion in *Yoma*, but is implicit in the verse; after God bears the *avon* and *pesha* as though they were just as a *ḥata'a,* He bears the *ḥata'a* itself. The sequence is therefore arranged from *avon* to *ḥata'a,* because the person's soul is the last item repaired. First God repairs goodness, followed by kingship and then, finally, the human being.

TOWARDS FORGIVENESS

Sins, as we have noted, are compared to stains. *Noseh Ḥata'a* protects the body so that it does not become polluted by the filth on the garment. The stain remains, but it does not harm the person himself. Atonement, on the other hand, demands sincere repentance and removes the stain entirely. As R. Akiva famously comments in the final Mishna in *Yoma*: "Who purifies you? Your Father in Heaven, as it says, '*Mikveh Yisrael HaShem*' (Jeremiah 17:13)." The cleansing, the removal of the stain, is reserved for Yom Kippur, when the process of repentance and atonement is completed: "For on this day He shall atone for you from all your sins; you shall be purified before the Lord" (Leviticus 16:30).

In this context, as regarding the other attributes, we speak of preserving existence, not atonement. In contrast to the previous attributes, however, we now speak not only of the existence of life as opposed to death, but of a healthy existence, an existence of spiritual force and capabilities. Nevertheless, even at this point, there is still some way to go before we reach *kapara,* the complete removal of the stain.

The Talmud Yerushalmi (*Shavuot* 1:6) suggests interpreting *Noseh Avon* as though it were written "*nosheh avon,*" implying that the sin is forgotten. Yet we have previously encountered the Yerushalmi's comment, "Whoever says that the Almighty 'yields' – his intestines shall be yielded." The Almighty does not simply "give in" and forego, and He certainly does not forget. It seems to me that the Yerushalmi here refers to the Almighty's casting of sin into the abyss of forgetfulness; He turns it into something of no significance. This means that, as we explained, the sin will have no effect upon the individual or upon the world; it will be like something altogether forgotten because it has no substance. Sin loses its weight, its color, and becomes transparent; it dissipates like a cloud and departs like a passing breeze – not so that we need not assume responsibility for it, but rather so that we can continue existing with a whole soul. It is only after we regain our full spiritual capacity that we can assume responsibility and repent.

There are two stages in the Thirteen Attributes, reflected in the division in the Torah between two verses. From "*HaShem HaShem*" through "*Rav Ḥesed VeEmet*," we deal with the evaluation, the weighing of the person's merits against his demerits, and how the scales will be turned in his favor. The essence of these attributes relates to the power of goodness to overpower evil. When we reach *Notzer Ḥesed LaAlafim*, a new verse begins – and with it a new stage in the process of divine mercy. The essence of the attributes at this stage is dealing with evil itself, neutralizing and repairing it. The attributes of *Noseh Avon VaFesha VeḤata'a* continue this second stage: "Do not just keep me alive, but also cure me. Do not only preserve existence, but preserve the completion of goodness, divine kingship, and the soul."

As we have noted numerous times, we carry the Almighty's name and serve as the "chariot" for the *Shekhina*'s presence in the world. Reciting the Divine Attributes of Mercy strengthens the *Shekhina*'s presence, in particular *within ourselves*, upon our shoulders. This closeness, this identification, sustains the individual and also cures him. In light of this, we might suggest a new meaning to the expression we encountered at the outset: "The Almighty wrapped Himself as a *shali'aḥ tzibbur*…" God does not stand opposite us, listening to what we say. *Seliḥot* are effective because He stands among us, serving as our prayer leader. As a result of this connection, we are told, "They shall perform this service before Me and I shall forgive them." The forgiveness comes from within, from my soul's attachment to its source. The *tallit* worn by the Almighty covers us and joins us with the *shali'aḥ tzibbur*, together with all *Am Yisrael*.

Chapter Nine

VeNakeh

The thirteenth and final Divine Attribute of Mercy is "*VeNakeh,*" "And Cleanses." After describing God as "*Noseh Avon VaFesha VeḤata'a,*" the Torah concludes, "*venakeh lo yenakeh.*" According to the simple meaning of the text, "*VeNakeh*" is not actually an Attribute of Mercy at all. In fact, it appears to be quite the opposite; it limits the extent of the Attributes of Mercy that precede it.

In Biblical Hebrew, the use of a double verb expresses emphasis or an extreme manifestation of the verb. Thus, "*sakol yisakel*" (Exodus 19:13) means, "he shall surely be stoned," and "*ha'anek ta'anik*" (Deut. 15:14) means, "you shall surely grant." Conversely, the negation of a double verb (in the form of "[verb] *lo* [verb]") implies that the action will certainly not occur. Accordingly, the phrase "*nakeh yenakeh*" would mean, "He shall surely cleanse," and the phrase "*venakeh lo yenakeh*" means, "He shall surely not cleanse."

"*Venakeh lo yenakeh*" emphasizes that notwithstanding everything that has been said until this point regarding the extent of God's mercy, He will certainly not cleanse the sinner entirely. Despite the Divine Attributes of Mercy, the attribute of Justice demands retribution, and a sin is not erased entirely. Indeed, God even punishes children for their fathers' sins when they continue to follow in their fathers' evil ways.[1]

Accordingly, there appear to actually be only twelve Attributes of Mercy, and the recitation of the Attributes in the framework of the *Seliḥot* service clearly differs from the simple meaning of the verse. By including the word "*VeNakeh*," we not only abridge the verse, but actually reverse the meaning of the word! We transform "*venakeh lo yenakeh*," which means that God will certainly *not* cleanse the sin entirely, into "*VeNakeh*," that God *will* cleanse the sin. How could *Ḥazal* create an attribute in direct opposition to what is written in the Torah?

This is not only an exegetical-textual question, but a halakhic one as well. The Gemara teaches that "we do not parse any verse that Moses did not parse" (*Berakhot* 12b; *Ta'anit* 27b). We are not permitted to divide verses in the Torah differently than they are traditionally read. Certainly, then, we may not read a verse in a manner that directly contradicts its true meaning!

The answer to this question – which also holds the key to understanding this attribute – is that the content of this verse is revealed twice. The original source of the Attributes of Mercy is a verse in *Parashat Ki Tisa*, and thus constitutes part of the revelation of the Torah, which was given at Mount Sinai. That verse indeed presents only twelve attributes of mercy, which were bound by a strict limitation – "*venakeh lo yenakeh*." The Attributes of Mercy can in no way erase the sin entirely. But we find another revelation of the Attributes of Mercy, one which occurred not in the public, overt revelation of God to *Benei Yisrael*, but rather in the *nikrat hatzur* ("cleft of the rock"), in hiding, with covered face, an intimate secret conversation of the Holy One with His trusted servant whom He favored, and to whom He disclosed His name. When God revealed the attributes to Moses in the *nikrat hatzur*, He revealed an additional attribute – the thirteenth attribute. This attribute is hidden and even denied in the Torah. But in this revelation at the *nikrat hatzur*, God did not speak to Moses "face to face, as a man speaks to his fellow,"

1. This is essentially the same concept articulated in the Talmud Yerushalmi regarding the attribute of *Erekh Apayim*; God is "*ma'arikh af vegavi dilei*" – He delays His anger, and then collects what is His.

but rather "wrapped Himself like a *shali'aḥ tzibbur*," covering His face and head, as it were, and called out the Attributes. When we recite *Seliḥot*, we do not cite a verse from the Torah, but rather reenact the vision revealed to Moses, regarding which God said to Moses, "They shall perform this service before Me and I shall forgive them." "This service" – meaning, from "*HaShem, HaShem*" through and including "*VeNakeh*." It is indeed forbidden to cite verses in a distorted form; here, however, in the *Seliḥot* service, we do not quote a verse from the Torah given at Sinai. We rather recreate the encounter at the *nikrat hatzur*.

Ḥazal themselves noted that these two revelations essentially contradict one another (*Yoma* 86a):

> R. Elazar says: It cannot say "*venakeh*," because it already says, "*lo yenakeh*," but it cannot say "*lo yenakeh*," because it already says, "*nakeh*." How is this possible? He cleanses those who repent and does not cleanse those who do not repent.

In the Gemara's presentation, the troubling contradiction is not between two different verses or even two parts of the same verse, but rather between the two different revelations of the Almighty's attributes – God is both *nakeh* and *lo yenakeh*. The Gemara resolves this contradiction by pointing to repentance as the determining factor – "He cleanses those who repent and does not cleanse those who do not repent." Repentance leads to the revelation of the thirteenth Attribute of Mercy, *VeNakeh*, from amidst the attribute of Justice, "*nakeh lo yenakeh*."

THE LIMITS OF MERCY

We have noted repeatedly that the Divine Attributes of Mercy are not predicated upon *teshuva*. Repentance is a goal of divine mercy, not a prerequisite. The Attributes of Mercy enable existence in the current condition of a sinner who has yet to repent so that *teshuva* can eventually be achieved. For example, the attribute of *Erekh Apayim* delays the punishment for sin in the hope that by the time that punishment is ready to surface, the individual will have already performed *teshuva*. The Attributes of Mercy allow the world to exist *despite* the occurrence of sin.

According to *Ḥazal* (*Bereshit Raba* 39), Abraham articulated the necessity of God's mercy in his appeal to spare the condemned city of Sodom:

> R. Levi said: "Shall the Judge of the earth not perform justice?" [Genesis 18:25] – If You want a world, then there cannot be judgment, and if You want judgment, then there cannot be a world. How can You grasp the cord from both sides? You want a world and You want judgment! Choose one, but if You refuse to relent even a bit, the world cannot exist.

The world cannot exist when the attribute of Justice reigns supreme. The world is full of sins and sinners, and God, who is good, desires a perfect world; if the divine will could not tolerate sin at all, the world could not exist. The Divine Attributes of Mercy essentially expand the divine will to include even our corrupted world and allow for its existence.

Since the Attributes of Mercy allow the existence of sin, there is no apparent existential need for its elimination. If the world can continue to exist even with the filth of sin, why do we require the attribute of "cleansing"? It would seem that complete atonement for sin is a gift that God grants His people, a precious goal achieved through the detailed procedures of the Yom Kippur service and the sacrifices, but nevertheless a concept that the world could survive without. Indeed, the entire purpose of the Attributes of Mercy is to allow people the opportunity to exercise their free will, to present the option of sinning just as they have the option of performing good deeds, and then to ultimately bear responsibility for their actions. Accordingly, God is *Raḥum, Ḥanun, Erekh Apayim, Rav Ḥesed VeEmet* – but "*nakeh lo yenakeh*." He does not cleanse sins entirely.

However, in the final attribute, the attribute of *VeNakeh*, an additional existential need is revealed. The basis of this attribute is the assertion that it does not suffice to accept a world that includes sin – not even with the expectation of future perfection. The person demands also "cleansing" – because for him, this is an existential need. Existence with sin, an existence in which I breathe, walk, eat and live, but find myself distant from God, without friendship, without dialogue – this is not existence at all. The twelve attributes guaranteed existence, but an existence of sin, of alienation and distance. Even *Noseh Avon VaFesha VeḤata'a,* which sought to prevent the injuries of sin to the soul, did not touch on the existence of the sin itself. The individual exists, he is even healthy, but he cannot be close to God. This is logically possible, according to the rationale that we have explained in discussing the previous attributes. But the individual is still not satisfied. In his eyes, this is intolerable. An existence far from the Almighty is not existence at all. Sin, even if it does not kill the violator, and even if it does not affect his spiritual capabilities, it nevertheless separates him from God. There cannot be any existential merging between God and sin.

This is expressed in the exchange between God and Moses after the sin of the golden calf. God said to Moses, "And so, go lead the nation to where I told you – behold, my angel will walk before you. And on the day of My accounting, I shall make an accounting of their sin for them" (Exodus 32:34). God's mercy tolerated the sin and enabled *Benei Yisrael* to continue to move forward, but the sin itself was not completely cleansed. Thus, "on the day of My accounting, I shall make an accounting." As a result, only His angel would accompany the people, as God cannot bond with sinners: "For I shall not go up [to the Land] in your midst" (ibid. 33:3). Moses responded, "If Your countenance does not go, do not take us up from here" (ibid. 33:15). Such an arrangement is worthless in Moses' eyes. Even if *Benei Yisrael* are allowed to continue towards *Eretz Yisrael,* even if the original plan remains in place despite the sin, Moses is unwilling to accept an arrangement in which God is not personally involved. If there is no connection to God, there is no reason to continue existing. No life plan can exclude God's "countenance."[2]

Despite all the benefits of the first twelve attributes, it is the final one – *VeNakeh* – that ensures that a sinner can regain meaning in his life through reconnection to God.

If so, why is this principle hidden and not revealed explicitly in the Torah? The answer is found in *Ḥazal*'s resolution of the contradiction between the two revelations of the Attributes – God cleanses those who repent, but not those who fail to. In the absence of *teshuva,* this attribute not only does not work – it does not exist at all. As long as a

2. For further exploration of this dialogue between God and Moses, see Appendix II.

man is satisfied with basic existence, with biological functioning alone, there is no need for *VeNakeh,* as he can continue to live through God's mercy alone. Only when a person feels that he cannot exist at a distance and attempts to draw close to God, is it revealed that he is, in fact, correct – man indeed cannot live distant from God. Only then must the Divine Attributes of Mercy provide a solution for his existential problem.

Thus, repentance is not a precondition for the attribute of *VeNakeh,* but rather reveals it and brings it into reality. In the world of *teshuva,* there can be neither justice nor mercy without the cleansing of sin. Repentance alters the very definition of what existence is, and consequently changes the solution to the problem of human existence. Before he repents, man survives on mercy alone. Once he repents and realizes his sorry spiritual state, the covenant of creation must provide a solution for his alienation from God. When alienation is an existential problem – and for the *ba'al teshuva,* it genuinely is so – then the Creator who desires the continued existence of His world must reveal the attribute of *VeNakeh.*[3]

In the inanimate world, two objects can become closer to one another simply by moving one towards the other. In human relationships, however, a gap cannot be closed by one party drawing near without a corresponding gesture made by the other. Regardless of which side should initiate this process,[4] it must occur bilaterally, with both sides drawing

---

3. In the first chapter, we noted that the "order of *Seliḥot*' parallels the "order of prayer." The Thirteen Attributes of Mercy parallel the thirteen middle blessings of the *Shemoneh Esreh,* the thirteen requests made in every prayer. Originally, there were only twelve middle blessings and requests (and the complete prayer had only eighteen blessings, thus lending the name "*Shemoneh Esreh*"). The sages in Yavne added an additional request – the *Birkhat HaMinim,* a request for the extirpation of heretics and the destruction of the kingdom of evil. Similarly, there are only twelve "original" Attributes of Mercy; the thirteenth is revealed only through the repentance of one who seeks to live in a world without any sin or evil at all. The attribute of *VeNakeh* is thus parallel to *Birkhat HaMinim,* which was also revealed only in response to the desire for the elimination of evil: "Let the informers have no hope, and all the heretics shall be lost." The original version of the prayer reflects the Torah of Sinai; the expanded version reflects the revelation of the *nikrat hatzur.*
4. *Ḥazal* (*Eikha Raba* 5:21) famously comment that *Knesset Yisrael* say, "Bring us back to You, and we shall return," while the Almighty says, "Return to Me, and I shall

closer to one another. Similarly, as long as there is no awakening on *Am Yisrael*'s part, there is no meaning to God's drawing closer. When God gave us the Torah, he "forced [it] on Israel like a barrel;" He descended to the people upon Mount Sinai without any initiative on their part. Thus, the element of "cleansing" is absent from the attributes revealed in the Torah. *Benei Yisrael*'s initiative of *teshuva,* expressed in Moses' demand for God's closeness, introduced and revealed a new existential need – the need for closeness to God. Until that point, we managed fine with existence in accordance with God's will; now, we demanded existence with God's love. *VeNakeh* therefore appears in God's revelation of His attributes to Moses after *Benei Yisrael* have done *teshuva.*

According to what we have said, cleansing of sin – correcting the situation rather than simply preserving it – is not an element of God's special covenant with Israel. In fact, it is part of His covenant for the world's existence – but this covenant is necessary only for those who repent. When man declares, "If Your countenance does not go, do not take us up from here," then – and only then – the "hidden" attribute of *VeNakeh* emerges from out of "*nakeh lo yenakeh.*"

When a person is aroused to *teshuva* – when he understands that he cannot live in a world where God's hand does not guide and protect him, where he does not hear the Almighty's whispers, and where he does not feel the light of God's countenance upon his face – then his existential desperation gives rise to the revelation of the *Shekhina* and the revelation of a new attribute.

There is nothing novel in the concept of man's actions serving as the basis for a new divine revelation. This is, in fact, the basic notion underlying the *Seliḥot,* as we discussed in our introduction. What is new here is that man's act of *teshuva,* and not merely invoking the Attributes, is what *initiates* the attribute, rather than simply giving it a basis. If one is not aroused to draw close to the Almighty, and nevertheless calls out the attribute of *VeNakeh,* the attribute simply will not exist for him, despite the covenant God made with the Thirteen Attributes and despite the

---

then return to you." In either case, however, unilateral movement of one without the other does not suffice. "Bring us back to You" must be followed by "and we shall return."

general concept of God's revelation in response to the person's calling that attribute. In order for *VeNakeh* to exist at all, there must first be an existential need for divine closeness. Only then does the attribute of *VeNakeh* emerge from the midst of the *nikrat hatzur.*

Teshuva is not a precondition of kindness; it rather creates a new world, a world of repentance, a world in which a new attribute of kindness is an existential necessity and is thus revealed in response to the individual's *teshuva.*

How does the attribute of *VeNakeh* work? The meaning of *nakeh* indicates that the sin itself is cleansed and dissipated, as though it never were. Of course, this too depends on the power of *teshuva.* Through repentance, the world of man changes, and the man himself is transformed. It is not *teshuva* itself which cleanses man, but the graciousness of the Creator. "Return to Me, and I shall return to you." Narrowing the gap between myself and the source of life, the closeness and the newfound intimacy, that is what washes away the existence of sin. A man repents – his soul yearns for the attribute of *VeNakeh,* for a return unto God – and God returns to him and the presence of the *Shekhina* in his life fills the void and negation that the sin had opened in his existence. Repentance gives birth to a new world – a world where it is impossible to exist without intimacy with God. The return of God creates a new world - a world where man is cleansed of sin.

This attribute guarantees not only survival, but closeness; not simply existence with the sin, but rather its elimination, cleansing and atonement. Therefore, allow me - for the last time - to suggest yet another explanation for the Almighty's "wrapping Himself like a *shaliaḥ tzibbur.*" The thirteenth attribute is based upon closeness and togetherness. When we feel a yearning that can find no rest, the feeling that without His closeness there can be no life at all, then the Almighty does not stand opposite us, at a distance, granting us life, but rather lives among us. "Like a hind longs at the streams of water, so does my soul long for You, O God!" (Psalms 42:2). When Divine closeness becomes like water for the thirsty, and life with sin feels like strangulation, when one senses that he cannot live without God, then a covenant is made with the thirteenth attribute and guarantees that God will indeed draw close by cleansing the sin.

But since we still deal here with an existential attribute, this is not the end of the process. "Cleansing" marks but the preliminary stage in the process of atonement and purification. This cleansing allows for divine closeness. The world of repentance, the world of closeness, is now made possible. God promises more than that – the process of Yom Kippur, the day on which He grants atonement and purification. Purification demands more than simply feeling the need for closeness; it demands immersing oneself in the waters of renewal. The basic existence of closeness is achieved through the completion of the Thirteen Attributes. But God's covenant with Israel gives more than just existence; it gives purification before God. After the attribute of *VeNakeh* granted to those who repent, a Jew must continue forward in order to be a bearer of the covenant, in order to be a builder of sanctity. On the day that is spent in its entirety "*lifnei HaShem*" ("before the Lord"), on the Day of Atonement, we will perfect and serve, sacrifice and prostrate ourselves, repent in complete *teshuva*, and be privileged to greet our King in complete purity.

Appendix 1

Davar Shebikedusha

As we noted in the introduction, the recitation of *Seliḥot* as part of the prayer service is not explicitly mentioned in the Talmud, although it is based on an *aggadic* statement (*Rosh HaShana* 17b).

As an organized prayer, *Seliḥot* first appear in the siddurim of the Geonim. The Tur (*Oraḥ Ḥayyim* 565) writes in the name of R. Natan Gaon that an individual is not permitted to recite *Seliḥot* without a *minyan* of ten. The Tur himself does not cite a reason, but the *Siddur R. Amram Gaon*, the source for R. Natan's ruling, writes:

> For when the community congregates, and they fast, and perform acts of charity, and plead for mercy, and dedicate their hearts to their Father in Heaven, then the Holy One, Blessed be He, has mercy on them, and does not despise the prayer of the many, and He answers them, as is written, "For God is mighty and does not despise." God has made a covenant with Moses our teacher and with our fathers that they [the Thirteen Attributes] do not return unanswered, as is written, "Behold, I am making a covenant," and therefore they may only be recited within the community.

The implication of this statement is that since the recitation of the Thirteen Attributes of Mercy is based on a special covenant enacted between God and the Jewish People, it cannot be recited by an individual outside of the communal framework.

What is the halakhic basis for a prohibition on the recitation of a prayer by the individual? The only halakhic category that meets this criterion is that of *davar shebikedusha,* "a matter of holiness:" "A *davar shebikedusha* may not be recited by less than ten" (*Berakhot* 21a). This reasoning is stated explicitly by the Rashba (Responsa 1:211), who supports this conclusion by citing the description in the passage in *Rosh HaShana*: "This teaches us that God wrapped himself like a *shali'aḥ tzibbur* and said: Whenever Israel sins, let them recite this order and I shall forgive them." Since God is described as a *shali'aḥ tzibbur,* the implication is that there is a *tzibbur* in attendance. The Rashba concludes that the Thirteen Attributes must belong to the category of *davar shebikedusha,* as there is no other available explanation for why a prayer should be restricted to *tzibbur*.[5]

Why are the Thirteen Attributes, a list of names of God, considered to belong to this category, in the manner of the Kaddish or the prayer known as *Kedusha*? Unlike those prayers, there is no hint of the concept of *kedusha,* of holiness or sanctity, in the text of the Thirteen Attributes, and the Rashba's conclusion thus appears somewhat arbitrary.[6]

In order to understand why the Thirteen Attributes of Mercy have

5. The Mishna (*Megilla* 23b) lists the prayers that may only be recited with a *minyan,* and the Thirteen Attributes does not appear on that list. The Tashbetz (*Rosh HaShana* 17b) explains that the Mishna lists only mandatory prayers that are part of the established order of prayer, whereas *Seliḥot,* including the Thirteen Attributes, is not a mandatory prayer, but merely a recommendation of God to Moses. The Tashbetz writes that it is impermissible to recite the Attributes in a manner that differs from the divine example at the cleft in the rock, including the need for a *minyan* hinted to by the words, "He wrapped himself like a *shali'aḥ tzibbur*."
6. In fact, the Tur disagrees, concluding, "I do not understand what problem there is [in reciting the Attributes privately], as it is no more than the reading of a verse from the Torah; rather, the sages restricted only a *davar shebikedusha,* such as Kaddish, *Kedusha,* and *Barekhu*." The Tur assumes that the Thirteen Attributes are not a *davar shebikedusha* and that there is no other reason to avoid reciting them in private.

the status of a *davar shebikedusha*, we must first understand the special status of this type of prayer and why its recitation is restricted to a *tzibbur*.

THE NATURE OF *KEDUSHA*

Although, as we noted, the basic law applicable to the category of *devarim shebikedusha* is that a *minyan* of ten is required to recite them, Rabbeinu Yona, a Spanish commentator of the thirteenth century, remarks that this principle cannot be taken at face value:

> Undoubtedly, the recitation of the Shema is included in the category of *davar shebikedusha*, since there is no greater *davar shebikedusha* than the acceptance of the yoke of heaven ("*ol malkhut shamayim*"). Yet it is not subject to this law, as it may be recited in private.[7]

Why does Rabbeinu Yona assume that *Keriat Shema*, the recitation of the verse, "Hear O Israel, HaShem our God, HaShem is one," is not only a *davar shebikedusha*, but the *davar shebikedusha* par excellence?

The defining aspect of *Keriat Shema*, in Rabbeinu Yona's view, is "*kabbalat ol malkhut shamayim*." When we recite the verse of Shema, we are accepting upon ourselves the kingship of God. According to Rabbeinu Yona, there are two kinds of *devarim shebikedusha* – those that require a *minyan* and those that do not – but both are exemplified by Shema. This is the key to understanding the concept of *davar shebikedusha*.

As we stressed in the introduction, in Jewish thought, the kingship of God is not understood as a static, absolute state. We are charged with the job of creating the kingship of God by accepting His rule upon ourselves – "There cannot be a king without a people." The attribute of kingship is by definition a relative one. While it is true that in the absolute sense, God is King as an aspect of His absolute existence, in another sense, God is only King in relation to the world, to people who accept His rule and abide by His will. God is "*Adon olam asher malakh beterem kol yetzir nivra*" – the Master of the world, who ruled before any other

7. Talmidei Rabbeinu Yona, *Berakhot* 12b.

creation came into existence – but *"le'et na'asah beḥeftzo kol, azai Melekh shemo nikra"* – it was when He created the world that He was officially designated as King.

God's kingship is, in fact, the theme of our Rosh HaShana prayers, in which we anticipate the day when God will be King over all, even as we declare that He has always been King. More importantly, on Rosh HaShana we actively crown God as our King, and by doing so, we add qualitatively and quantitatively to His kingship. The sages describe the blowing of the *shofar* as an act of coronation; God ascends, as it were, His throne, which can only be established by His willing subjects.

Although this concept is illustrated most clearly by God's attribute of kingship, it is not limited to kingship. All of God's attributes exhibited within the world (as opposed to their absolute aspect) are dependent on the world and on the acts of people. If no one turns to God, then He is absent. If no one calls on His name, then His name is not found, and He is not present. While God, in His absolute transcendence, is wholly independent of the world, His presence in the world is dependent on a vehicle, on someone who will bear His honor and glory. The sages describe Abraham as having "mended the rift" because he "called on the name of God" in a world where God had previously been absent. As paradoxical as it may sound, the absolute and supremely transcendent God is dependent on our blessing when He relates to this world.

My master and teacher, R. Yosef Dov Soloveitchik *z"l*, explained that this is the meaning of the formula of all *berakhot*. "Blessed are You, our God, King of the world" means that we indeed add power and glory to the presence of God by discovering Him and recognizing Him in the world. In the act of prayer, we turn to God to receive everything from the One who needs nothing from us, but from whom we need everything. That very act itself becomes an act of giving to God, of increasing His presence and glory, of adding to His holy name. Indeed, Psalm 114 opens, "*Barekhi nafshi et HaShem*" – "My soul, bless God" – and immediately continues, "HaShem my God, You grow very great; You are clothed with beauty and majesty."

This is the meaning of *kedusha*, of holiness in this world. God told the Jewish People, "I shall be sanctified in the midst of the children of Israel" (Leviticus 32:22). Holiness implies the presence of God, and therefore does not apply to any other being. A place, a time, or a person is holy only because it bears the name of God, because through it the name of God is revealed and the presence of God is strengthened. When we recite a *davar shebikedusha,* as audacious as it sounds, we add to His revealed holiness by imbuing the world with His holiness; we increase the revealed presence of God.

The Kaddish begins, "*Yitgadal veyitkadash shemei raba*" – "May His great name be sanctified and magnified." It is a cardinal belief of Judaism that God can be made greater, or rather, that His name can be made greater. When this takes place, *kedusha* ensues, for holiness is the increase in the presence of God in the world.

This aspect of God, God-in-the-world, is referred to by the sages as the "name" of God. A name is what someone is called by others; the name of God, as opposed to God Himself, is thus God's presence in people's mouths. This reference is made in Kaddish, when we say, "May His great name be blessed forever." God's presence in the world is also referred to as "*kevod HaShem,*" God's honor or glory, for honor is something that appears in reflection, something given by others. We use this term in *Kedusha* when we say that "His honor fills the world." Finally, the concept of God's manifestation in the world is referred to as "*malkhut,*" kingship. Thus, *Kedusha* concludes with the exclamation, "God shall rule forever, your God, Zion, for generation upon generation."

In *Keriat Shema,* which, as we saw, is also thematically a *davar shebikedusha,* we find all three terms used together, as we recite after the line of Shema: "Blessed be the NAME of the HONOR of his KINGSHIP forever."

THE NEED FOR A *MINYAN*

Now that we have established the meaning of the category of *devarim shebikedusha,* we must consider why some of these prayers, such as *Kedusha,*[8] require a *minyan,* while others, like Shema, do not.

The requirement of a *minyan* is derived from the verse we quoted above: "I shall be sanctified in the midst of the children of Israel"

8. "*Kedusha*" refers to the verses, "Holy, Holy, Holy, God of Hosts; the world is full of His glory" and "Blessed be the glory of God from His place."

(Leviticus 32:22). The process of adding to the revealed *kedusha* of God and realizing the immanence of God's presence in the world – the process accomplished through *devarim shebikedusha* – must be done in the midst of the community. The job of supporting God's presence is given to *Knesset Yisrael,* not to the individual Jew, and a *minyan* of ten represents the Jewish People as a whole.

In contrast, when I recite the Shema, I am not directly creating the majesty of God. The purpose of the Shema is directed inward – a Jew has the duty to daily reaffirm his loyalty to the King. Shema is a sort of "pledge of allegiance." Although the act of acceptance of God's rule automatically contributes to the reality of His rule, the purpose of the recitation of Shema is not to act upon God's presence, but to affirm my duty, my ability, and my opportunity to create *kedusha* in the world. Every mitzva I perform brings about an increase in the presence of God and actualizes *kedusha* in myself, but a *davar shebikedusha* in the formal halakhic sense, such as *Kaddish* and the *Kedusha,* is the relatively rare act of directly affirming my duty, my ability, and my opportunity to create *kedusha,* to actually increase *kedusha.*

If, as we explained the words of R. Yona, *devarim shebikedusha* are divided into descriptive recitations and constructive recitations, between "Shema-types" and "*Kedusha*-types," it is clear that the *Seliḥot* are a classic example of the latter. In fact, their recitation is nearly meaningless without the constructive element. As we have emphasized repeatedly, the purpose of *Seliḥot* is to increase the power of the Attributes of Mercy by increasing the presence of the merciful *Shekhina* in the world. The very recitation of the Thirteen Attributes of Mercy is a magnification and sanctification of God's name in the world that He created. Without the creative sanctification of the *Seliḥot,* without the element of covenant, we have no more than a list of names and attributes. Only by reciting them as God recited them before Moses in the cleft of the rock, when He wrapped himself like a *shali'aḥ tzibbur,* does one endow them with the significance of prayer.

This idea lies at the root of the disagreement in the halakha concerning the recitation of the Thirteen Attributes in private. The *Posekim* permit reciting the text of the *Kedusha* if it is done descriptively, if one is merely recounting how the angels recite *Kedusha*.[9] Accordingly, the Rashba rules, in the same responsa cited above, that an individual may recite the Thirteen Attributes "in the manner of a simple reading," as if reading the verse from the Torah. A *minyan* is only necessary when they are recited "in the manner of a prayer and request."[10]

The Baḥ (565) disagrees with this ruling, however, arguing that it is impossible to recite the Thirteen Attributes without intending it as a prayer and a request. The Thirteen Attributes have no meaning in the framework of prayer if they are not, by their very recitation, establishing and deepening the presence of the Attributes of Mercy and graciousness in the divine conduct of the world. This is unlike the recitation of the *Kedusha*, in which we praise God, and which therefore can be recited as a description of the way that the angels praise God. There is no parallel meaning in the *Seliḥot*; the only possible intent of the recitation of the Thirteen Attributes is to activate the covenant of the Thirteen Attributes.

According to our explanation, the Baḥ's approach is clear. The covenant of the Thirteen Attributes of Mercy constitutes the enthronement of God. If God is our King, He rules over us, and if He is a merciful and gracious God, then His divinity is revealed over us in that manner. The only way to recite the Attributes without being involved in a *davar shebikedusha* would be to intend that God not reveal Himself to us as a merciful and gracious God – and that is certainly an implausible intent for one reciting *Seliḥot*!

TALKING *KEDUSHA* AND LIVING *KEDUSHA*

In the chapter on the attribute of *Rav Ḥesed*, we noted that every mitzva that an individual performs carries within it the presence of the *Shekhina*, and that is the added weight – the *Rav Ḥesed* – given to good over evil

9. Many authorities claim that the *Kedusha* found before the morning Shema and in *UVa LeTziyon* are descriptive, and not constructive. These prayers simply recount what the angels recite, which is precisely why they may be recited in private.
10. In order to make it clear that one is reciting the attributes as a verse and not as a prayer, the Terumat HaDeshen (8) suggests reading it with the cantillation of the Torah reading.

when one is weighed against the other. In the chapter on the attribute of *Emet,* we argued that the movement of man towards God, his aspiration to come closer to God, is itself the this-worldly reflection of the perfection of God; it is itself the Divine Presence in the world and the basis for holiness. The "seal of God," the attribute of Truth, arises out of the ground of the creation of man. We enthrone God through the very act of living "Jewishly," by following the path of mitzvot and living according to the Torah. Why, then, do we need *devarim shebikedusha,* verbal recitations such as *Kedusha,* Kaddish, *Barekhu,* and the Thirteen Attributes, to accomplish the same goal?

Moreover, there is a distinct difference between the two paths of sustaining holiness in the world. The verbal path, based on the content of prayer, is limited to community, as a *davar shebikedusha* requires a *minyan.* The path of mitzvot and action, on the other hand, is open to the individual and does not require a *minyan.* Every action performed by an individual in the service of God has a dimension of the enthronement of God and the grounding of holiness, and each man's path towards God is itself a divine presence. Why does verbal sanctification require a *minyan,* while the sanctification of actions does not?

The answer to this question will illuminate the principle of holiness in the world, while at the same time explicating the practical difficulty in fulfilling the principle.

As we have noted repeatedly, the principle that man is created in the image of God entails that man has the capacity to transcend his present natural state; the potential to be like God is an essential defining element of his nature. Man was created not to be man, but to be God, and although he cannot ever achieve that goal in actuality, he fulfills it by advancing and growing towards it. This self-transcendence, the progress and ascent on the ladder of existence, the coming closer to God and to the divine ideal which is the true form of man, is itself the presence of the *Shekhina* in the world. On the one hand, divinity is always necessarily beyond man, and is always separate and transcendent above the world; on the other hand, as measured by the process rather than by the state, the ascent of man towards the divine is itself the divine, as it reflects perfection by perfecting itself. The perfecting of man is the form that the perfection of God takes in the imperfect world.

The midrash reflects this idea in its comment on the verse, "Know that HaShem is God, He made us and we are to Him" [Psalms 100:3]: "He made us, and to Him we perfect our souls."[11]

The halakhic definition of holiness is "belonging to God." In what sense does man belong to God? The answer, the midrash says, is that man is directed towards God, just as the sacrifice is directed to God when it is offered on the altar. However, man is not directed towards God because he will be given to God, but because God is the goal of his existence – in other words, because God is the image in which he is created. We are "to Him" – for "to Him" we perfect our souls.

A great danger lies at the foot of this awesome vision. The distinction between the holiness of God in the actions of man and actual idolatry is very fine, almost microscopic. To say that man is God is idolatry; to say that man is the image of God is the essence of the service of God in Judaism. In the soul of every person who serves God lurks the danger of passing from one to the other. As soon as one begins to sense the presence of the *Shekhina* within himself – and the *Shekhina* is identical with his very existence as one who is in the process of transcending himself, as I have emphasized – he is liable to view himself as God.

There are many historical examples of this idolatrous corruption of the great doctrine of the image of God. The danger is always present, as the inner sense of the *Shekhina* is so seductive. Yet the difference between the two definitions is not between two parallel states, but between a state in actuality and a state of future potentiality. Man can genuinely be said to be divine, but only from the point of view of the process. In other words, he is never actually God, but only moves and develops towards God. Since the holiness of man derives from his dynamic connection to God as his goal, as soon as that connection is broken – as soon as man detours off the road that climbs towards the heavens – he becomes equal only to himself. In that static state, he leads a deficient, finite, and intrinsically limited existence, different only in degree from the existence of the rest of the natural world and from the animals created on the same day as he.

The *Shekhina* is present in man only as process, as potential, within

11. *Bereshit Raba* 100:1.

a dynamic continuum that includes his future and not only his present static state. A man engaged in self-perfection creates holiness, but this holiness must maintain a constant relationship with the transcendent holiness above. If one stops to weigh the holiness, to quantify it as it is now, it loses its sanctity, having severed its connection to the transcendent and absolute holiness of God. Thus, one who desires to be the base of the *Shekhina* must constantly connect to the transcendent holiness.

Man's actions create holiness that is rooted in him, while the recitation of a *davar shebikedusha* creates holiness rooted in God. The content of actions is man; the content of prayer is God. In both cases, the holiness is a result of man magnifying the presence of God. But the first, in the absence of a connection to the transcendent, will turn into the merely human; the second, if not accompanied by a constant striving on the part of man to transcend himself and climb to God, will free itself of its source in man and return to God from where it derives. In order that there be holiness rooted in the world and in man, perfection in the imperfect and constant perfecting, it is necessary that the holiness created by man be connected with its source and goal. This connection requires an explicit verbal recitation that sanctifies a man *unto* his creator – "May His great name be blessed forever and for all eternities."

> God immediately consulted the Torah, whose name is "Strength," to create the world. She answered Him and said: Master of the Universe, if the king has no army and he has no camp, over what shall he rule? And if there is no people to praise the king, what honor of the king is there?[12]

The actions of man in the service of God are the army and the camp of the king. In this case, every individual and every action has significance and stands alone. The praise of man and verbal sanctification, on the other hand, are the honor of the king, and honor requires a congregation, a people, for there is no king and no kingdom without a people. The first has its locus in the soul of man, and therefore it is sufficient to have one soul created in the image of God. The second has its locus

12. *Pirkei DeRabbi Eliezer* 3

in the presence of God over man, and therefore requires a base for the God, King of heaven and earth. That can only be accomplished among the congregation of Israel. *Shekhina* which is myself, I myself can create; *Shekhina* which is the King, only the people can create.

The presence of the *Shekhina,* the "King within me" or my self-transcendence reflecting His transcendent kingdom, is possible only by combining the two factors. Man's ability to bear the *Shekhina* is dependent on his being part of the People of Israel, a body that permanently bears the honor of the transcendent *Shekhina,* in which case the ascendance of each individual is directed to the transcendent objective that is the source of all holiness. Without the congregation, the efforts of the individual would turn towards self-service, to idolatry. Both in the consciousness of the individual and in the metaphysical reality of the *tikkun olam,* there must be a mutual connection between the sanctification of God's name in the world and the ascent of man towards God.

Appendix II

Restoring the Covenant

To complete our discussion of the Thirteen Attributes of Mercy, let us examine their broader original context – the negotiations between Moses and God in the aftermath of the sin of the golden calf. That dialogue, in which Moses strives to restore the relationship between God and the people of Israel, who had "turned aside quickly from the path which I had commanded them," climaxes with the revelation of the Thirteen Attributes and results in the formation of a new covenant. Thus, in their original context, the Attributes are part of the process of absolution necessary after the sin.

Our analysis will focus on a rather long section, from Exodus 32:7 until the end of the *parasha* (35:35). We notice immediately that there are several distinct stages in the narrative, with Moses returning several times to argue and pray before God.

I.

1. God: ""God tells Moses that the Jews – "Your people" – have destroyed and corrupted (*"shiḥet"*) themselves by constructing and worshipping the *egel*. He therefore proposes to destroy them

all ("*va'akhalem*") and appoint Moses as the father of a new nation (32:7–10).

2. Moses pleads ("*Vayeḥal*") with God not to destroy the people –"Turn from Your fierce wrath and repent of the evil against Your people" – as doing so would lead to a desecration of God's name. Moses further reminds God of His covenant with the forefathers. (32:11–13).
3. God reconsiders (32:14).
4. Moses descends from the mountain, breaks the *luḥot,* destroys the *egel,* and proceeds to command the Levites to slay three thousand people (32:15–30).

II.

1. Moses ascends to God and asks for forgiveness: "... If You would bear their sin; and if not, erase me from the book which You have written (*meḥeni na misifrekha*)" (32:31–32).
2. God tells Moses that He will decide whom to erase; in the meantime, Moses is to lead the people to their destination, and "on the day of retribution, I will seek retribution for their sin." God then smites the people for making the *egel* (32:33–35).
3. God then tells Moses to go up "from here" with the people and go to the land of Abraham, Isaac, and Jacob, the land flowing with milk and honey (33:1–3).
4. Moses sets up the tent outside the camp (33:7–11).

III.

1. Moses turns to God and asks to be informed of "the ways of God" ("*hodi'eni na et derakhekha*"), arguing, "See, this nation is Your people" (33:12–13).
2. God answers, "My visage shall go and give you rest" (33:14).
3. Moses seems to repeat his request, and God answers that He agrees (33:16–17).

IV.

1. Moses again requests, "*hareni na et kevodekha*" (33:18).
2. God promises to do so, but only when Moses is hidden in the cleft

of the rock (*nikrat hatzur*) – "You will see My back, but My face may not be seen" (33:19–23).

3. Moses carves the second set of *luḥot* and ascends the mountain alone (34:1–4).
4. God reveals the Thirteen Attributes of Mercy (34:5–7).
5. Moses asks once again that God enter the midst of Israel and forgive their sins (34:8–9).
6. God answers that He will make a *brit,* with wondrous and awesome acts. This is followed immediately by a list of mitzvot (34:10–26).

V.

Moses once again ascends the mountain for forty days to receive the second *luḥot.* When he returns, his face is glowing.

To properly understand this dialogue, we must explore the significance of each stage in the narrative. What is Moses requesting each time, and what is God's response?

A number of other elements in the narrative draw our attention as well. First, there seems to be a distinct sense of struggle between Moses, a solitary and lonely figure, and God, who only slowly concedes to Moses' requests. Furthermore, the national narrative – the quest for forgiveness for Israel – is interwoven with the personal story of Moses – his request to be shown "*kevodekha*" and "*derakhekha*," the use of his own relationship with God to plead for Israel ("erase me from the book;" "I have found favor in Your eyes" [33:12; 33:16; 34:9]), the light of his face, and God's granting a measure of national atonement together with favor to Moses (34:10, and especially 34:27).

We can understand the progression of this dialogue if we identify three distinct goals of Moses as he approaches God after the sin of the golden calf.

PREVENTING DESTRUCTION

Moses' first goal is to avert the destruction of the Jewish People, whom God had proposed to "eliminate" ("*va'akhalem*" [32:10]).[13] Moses pleads on their behalf immediately after being informed of the sin and prospective punishment, even before descending to see the sin for himself; there is no reason to descend if the nation is marked for total destruction.

Moses presents God with a twofold argument. First, he argues that total destruction of the Jewish People will lead to a *ḥillul HaShem,* desecration of God's name, as the Egyptians will hear about the failure of the Jews in the desert and attribute it to God's weakness. Second, Moses reminds God of His promise to Abraham, Isaac, and Jacob.

Note that neither of these arguments is based on the merits of the people. They do not provide any means or method to answer the question of how God can forgive the people for their sin or how they can continue their divine mission in its wake. Since Moses' single goal is to avert punishment, he appeals to outside factors – the adverse effect on the image of God in the eyes of the nations and the merits of the forefathers and God's promise to them.

These arguments are indeed sufficient to avert the decree; God immediately agrees, without qualification and without even speaking to Moses: "God repented of the evil which He proposed to do to His people" (32:14). There is no act of grace, nor any contact between God and Moses – merely a silent agreement not to destroy the nation.

Moses then hurries down the mountain and halts the rites in which the Jews are engaged.[14] He completely destroys every remnant of the *egel,* grinding it into dust, and kills three thousand of the people, presumably the worst offenders.[15] Outwardly, at least, the people have

13. "*Va'akhalem*" implies total elimination, until nothing is left. Compare this with the promise at the end of the *tokheḥa,* the rebuke found later in Leviticus (26:44): "And yet for all that, when they shall be in the land of their enemies, I will not abhor them nor loath them, to eliminate them (*lekhalotam*), and to break my pact (*berit*) with them, for I am HaShem their God."
14. In order to do so, Moses breaks the *luḥot;* discussion of that act is beyond the scope of our discussion in this context.
15. The sages claim those killed had actively worshipped the *egel* in the presence of witnesses and with proper warning.

been cleansed of their sin. But Moses knows that averting punishment is the simplest of his tasks. Now that he has ended the episode of the worship of the *egel*, he must repair the relationship between God and the people: "Now I will ascend to God; perhaps I will atone ("*akhapera*") for your sin" (32:30).

FORGIVENESS AND "BEARING" OF SIN

In the second stage, Moses turns to God with a new request: "And now, if You shall bear ("*tisa*") their sin; but if not, erase me from the book that You have written" (32:32).

A number of questions arise. First, of what book is Moses speaking? We naturally assume that he speaks of the Torah, but is it proper to refer to the Torah as a written book at this stage?[16] Second, is Moses' approach here not a bit too daring, even presumptuous? Most centrally, if Moses is going to seek atonement (*kapara*), as he promised the people, why does he ask for "bearing" of the sin (*nesiat ḥet*)? Precisely what does this term imply?

There are previous references in the Torah to "*nesiat ḥet*," but in those contexts, the phrase does not refer to forgiveness by God.[17] A sinner who does not merit forgiveness is said to "bear" his sin – for example, Cain says to God, "My sin is too great to bear (*mi'neso*)" (Genesis 4:13). By inference, if God is to "bear" the sin, His act is analogous to what the sinner would have done on his own were God not to help him. The sinner, such as Cain, suffers under the weight of his sin; "*nesiat ḥet*" means that God shares in that burden and shoulders, so to speak, part or all of its weight. This is not forgiveness as we generally understand it. Why is this new concept introduced here?

The sin of the *egel* is defined by God as a form of corruption or ruin – "*ki shiḥet amekha*" (Exodus 32:7). By turning away from God, the people corrupted themselves.[18] While God has repented of His intention

16. Of course, according to the midrash, the Torah existed before the creation of the world, but even midrashically, I am not sure that it was already *written*.
17. In Genesis 18:24, Abraham asks God to "bear" Sodom, but not to "bear" the sins of Sodom.
18. The people's rejection of God emerges from their declaration, "*Eileh Elohekha Yisrael*" – "This is your God, Israel, who has taken you out of Egypt." After all, the

to destroy them, which would have been a fitting punishment "measure for measure," it is still impossible for the original plan of the Exodus to continue as before. The state of the people is one of sin; they can no longer be God's people in such a state.

Moses thus asks that God somehow ameliorate the state of sin, somehow make it possible for Him to maintain His relationship with the people who have left Egypt, received the Torah, and are on the way to the Promised Land, even though these same people are still tainted and corrupted by their terrible transgression. He is asking God to "bear the sin," to tolerate it – not only in the sense of not acting against the sinners, but in actually remaining with them and maintaining His Holy Presence in their midst. If God maintains His relationship with the Jewish People in this state, He is, in effect, associating Himself with their sin; He is bearing the weight of the sin on Himself.

This request is audacious, nearly unthinkable. There is surely no precedent for such a relationship! God associated Himself with Abraham, Isaac, and Jacob because they bore His name and sanctified it. How can He place His name on a people who are desecrating it? The question is not moral, but metaphysical; the suggested combination of "*Am HaShem*" ("the People of God") and "worshippers of the *egel*" is a metaphysical contradiction, as is the combining of God with sin – "*noseh ḥet*!"

Moses, in fact, knows of no argument to justify such a novel and unthinkable condition. He therefore resorts to a "negative" argument – it may be true that You cannot rest Your Presence on this people, but in that case, You cannot rest it upon me either. This, I believe, is the meaning of the reference to the "book" that God has written. The only book mentioned so far in the Torah is the "*Sefer HaBerit*," the book written after Har Sinai that was the instrument of the covenant between God and the Jewish People (Exodus 24:7). The *Sefer HaBerit* was the means of establishing the connection between the Jews and God – they are God's people, and He is the God of Israel.[19] Moses thus says to God: If You are not willing to associate Your name with the Jewish People because

entire relationship of the people with God was previously defined by "I am your God, Who has taken you out of Egypt" (Exodus 20:2).

19. See Exodus 24:10: "They saw the God of Israel."

of what has happened, if You would erase them from the *Sefer HaBerit*, then erase my name from the book as well, for I, as a single individual, am not a partner in the *berit*. I too cannot bear the name of God; I too am a contradiction to the Holy Presence.

Moses is not trying to "blackmail" God. Rather, he is arguing that there must be a way for God to "bear sin," or else there would be no way to write the book at all. The book, the record of the Divine Presence, must be able to include sin; Moses is asking God to write the names of sinners in His book.

God's response is tantamount to refusal: "He who has sinned against Me, I will erase him from My book" (ibid. 32:33). God says that sinners against Him cannot be in the "book," although He is able to write it with others. God does give in a little to Moses, however: "Now go and lead the people to where I have told you … and on the day of retribution, I will seek retribution for their sins" (32:34). The program can go on, at least in the technical sense; the plan to continue to the Promised Land may proceed. But the name of the land is not mentioned, nor is there any reference to the *Avot* or God's promise to them. The plan continues, it seems, but without the inner meaning, without God's Presence. This, of course, was not what Moses had asked for.

The situation improves slightly after God smites those who had made the *egel*, when God tells Moses, "Go, ascend from here, you and the people whom you have brought out of Egypt, to *the land which I promised to Abraham, to Isaac, and to Jacob, saying, to your seed shall I give it…. To a land flowing with milk and honey* …" (33:1–3). A certain level of corruption has indeed been removed from the people, and Moses is told to leave that state of corruption behind – "Go, ascend from here." God now declares that the plan will continue with destiny, with meaning, according to the promise to the *Avot* and with a goal of arriving at the land flowing with milk and honey.

God has made it clear to Moses, however, that He will not be present in the midst of the Jewish People; an angel will go before them, but "I will not go up in your midst" (33:3). The people mourn when they hear these words (33:4), bemoaning the absence of God among them.[20] In a

20. See the Ramban's comments concerning the identity of this angel and the relation-

sharp and sensitive reading, the Ramban claims that the Jews understood that even the angel would be with them only "on the road," and not once they arrived in the Land. In other words, God has agreed to fulfill the promise, even referring to the Land directly, but not to continue beyond that. Once they reach *Eretz Yisrael,* the Jewish People will be a nation like any other. They will receive the outward fulfillment of the promise, but not the inner meaning. Moses has not finished his mission.

Moses now realizes something important: Although God has refused to rest His Presence amidst the people, He has indicated that Moses is still "in the book," that he is still a worthy carrier of the Divine Presence. Moses therefore removes his tent from the camp (33:6). In what appears to be an aside (33:7–11), we are told that the "pillar of cloud" representing the Divine Presence continues to rest on the tent whenever Moses is in it. In fact, anyone can "seek God" by going out of the camp to the tent (33:7). As a people, the Jews are still in the dark, but as individuals, the path is still open. In a beautiful depiction of nostalgic longing, we are told, "When Moses would go out to the tent, all the people would rise and stand, each at the entrance to his tent, and they would gaze after Moses, until he came into the tent.... And all the people saw the pillar of cloud stand at the tent entrance, and all the people rose and bowed, each at the entrance of his tent" (33:8–10). The people remained at the doors of their tents, gazing and bowing towards the distant figure of Moses, who meets God outside his tent. How can this gap be bridged? How can they return to their previous status in God's eyes?

BRIDGING THE GAP – A NEW *BERIT*

The third stage commences from this point, as Moses attempts to use the Presence of God that rests upon him as a bridge to all of Israel: "See, You have told me to take this people up, but You have not told me who will go with me" (33:12). God has, indeed, told Moses that it will be an angel that will lead the people, but Moses still refuses to accept that answer. "And You told me that You would know me by name, and that I have found favor in Your eyes...but see, this people is Your people." Essentially, Moses "traps" God (or God has set Himself up for a trap).

---

ship of between an "angel" and the presence of God.

You have told me to lead this people to the Promised Land, he tells God, but it is also clear that Your Presence rests upon me. If Moses continues to bear the Divine Presence, then the Divine Presence itself must be the guide of the unworthy Jews. Indeed, God answers tersely, "My face shall go and give you rest" (33:14).

Moses, emboldened by this forthright answer to his hinted request, repeats God's words, "If Your face will not go, do not take us from here" (33:15). In other words, there is no point in physically traveling to *Eretz Yisrael* if it is not part of the divine plan to rest His Presence on Israel. At this point, Moses makes his request explicit and includes the Jewish People as the recipients of Divine Presence: "How shall it be known that I have found favor in Your eyes, *I AND Your people,* if not by Your going with us; and we shall be distinguished (*veniflinu*), *I AND Your people,* from all the peoples on the face of the earth" (33:16).

Moses is not asking merely for help in reaching *Eretz Yisrael*; he is not satisfied with some gifts from God. He wants God Himself! This is implicit in the word "*niflinu*" – we shall be different, separated, and distinguished from all other peoples by the Presence of God in our midst.

This is followed by the episode of the "*nikrat hatzur,*" the cleft in the rock, and the revelation of the Thirteen Attributes. According to *Ḥazal,* each of these Attributes, at least up to the last one ("*Nakeh*"), deal with how God relates to sin – how He recreates the world with sin and despite sin – and not with *kapara,* atonement that follows repentance. In other words, God reveals to Moses the secret that he is looking for. This is summed up beautifully in one concise comment of *Ḥazal* that explains why God's name is repeated twice at the beginning of the list: "God before the sin, God after the sin" (*Rosh HaShana* 17b).

Moses responds to the revelation with one sentence: "If I have found favor in Your eyes God, God will go in our midst, and You will forgive our sins and transgressions, and grant us our inheritance" (Exodus 34:9). Moses has learnt the secret of "God after the sin." Before, he could only argue negatively – if You will not go with us, do not write my name and do not take us from here. Now, he knows that the names of God support his requests, and he immediately requests the Presence of God and, for the very first time, forgiveness.

God now answers in the affirmative: "I shall make a covenant"

(34:10). God promises a new *berit* to replace the old one – "I shall do marvels (*nifla'ot*), such as have never been created in all the earth and all the peoples." Rashi notes the striking similarity between the word "*nifla'ot*" and Moses' request for "*veniflinu*," that the Jewish People be distinguished from all other nations by the Presence of God in their midst. The presence of God among them, despite their sins, will be marked by wonders such as have never been seen, and they will be distinguished from all the peoples of the earth.

The content of the new *berit* between God and Israel follows this declaration. Why do these specific mitzvot constitute this *berit*? They seem to be a somewhat haphazard collection – the prohibition regarding forming pacts with the inhabitants of Canaan, the three pilgrimage festivals, the laws of the firstborn, Shabbat, the mitzva of pilgrimage to the Temple, two particular details of the *korban Pesaḥ*, laws regarding the first fruits, and the prohibition regarding mixing meat and milk.

If we are tempted to claim that no connection exists between this list and the preceding drama, the next section disabuses us of that notion, as Moses is commanded to write "these things, for on the basis of these things I have made a *berit* with you and with Israel" (34:27). This is the new *Sefer HaBerit,* which replaces the old one. Indeed, this list is nearly identical to the list at the end of *Parashat Mishpatim,* before Moses wrote the previous *Sefer HaBerit* (23:13–19). "God before the sin, God after the sin" – the content is the same, but how different it is when it applies to a world after sin, to a people who have been corrupted! The relationship is now the same – and completely different.

The content of this *berit,* these disparate mitzvot, has one common theme – these mitzvot impart the message that the effect is not completely determined by the cause, that the future is not merely the development of the past. In other words, although the people have indeed been corrupted by sin, this does not prevent the possibility of *kedusha* and *Shekhina* resting in their midst, and of their constituting an abode for God. These mitzvot warn the people not to perceive themselves as bound by their environment, by the ground from which they grow, but rather to always attempt to detach themselves from it and aspire upward.

The Torah is warning against the genetic fallacy, the idea that a thing is no more than the sum of its causes. Against the genetic fallacy stands the *kedusha* principle – wherever there is *kedusha,* the fruit can transcend the ground from which it grows. This principle is illustrated in all of the mitzvot in the new *berit.*

1. A series of prohibitions warning against forming a pact with the inhabitants of Canaan (34:12–17): God tells the people: You may be going into Canaan, but you will not be Canaanites. Note the language: "Lest you make a pact with the dwellers of the land onto which you are coming." You shall not assimilate with your environment.
2. Pesach, specifically eating the *matzot* (34:18): *Ḥametz,* leavened bread, represents natural development. *Matza* is unleavened; the natural process of growth has been halted. Freedom ("for in the month of the spring you left Egypt") requires the ability to break the natural chain.
3. The *bekhor* (firstborn) of both animals and human beings (34:19–20): A child is the product of his parents, and the firstborn is especially perceived as the inheritor, the continuation, of his parents. The halakha determines that the firstborn of any living thing is *kadosh,* holy, but this status is not natural; it is not inherited. The child is not only the product of his mother's womb.
4. Shabbat (34:21): Shabbat encompasses so many themes that it is easy to connect it to almost any idea. Note the context here, however: "Six days shall you work, but on the seventh day cease; during the plowing [season] and the harvest you shall cease." In this *parasha,* Shabbat is portrayed as an anti-agricultural law. Plowing and harvesting, working the land in order to bring forth its inherent potential, is negated one day a week.
5. Shavuot and Sukkot (34:22): Unlike in the context of Pesaḥ, no particular mitzva is mentioned here; we find only a command to celebrate the festivals, which are referred to in the agricultural context – the "first fruits of the wheat harvest" and the "festival of the ingathering." This verse serves as a prelude to the next verse, the mitzva of pilgrimage to the Temple, and its significance is clarified in that context.
6. *Aliya LeRegel* (34:23–24): Three times a year, a Jew is commanded

to tear himself away from home, field, and family[21] and travel to the seat of holiness to be seen before God. One may have a home, a place where one works the land, but one must be capable of leaving that home and ascending to God.

7. "You shall not slaughter My blood-offering while in the possession of *ḥametz*; nor may the Pesaḥ offering be left overnight until morning" (34:25): The Paschal lamb, the lamb of freedom, cannot exist alongside *ḥametz*, which, as we have seen, represents the product of natural growth and mechanical development. Similarly, the sacrifice may not be left over until morning; it is not a part of the natural world, left around to be savored when convenient.
8. *Bikkurim*, the first fruits (34:26): This mitzva constitutes the agricultural complement to the mitzvot related to the *bekhor* (firstborn). The fruit grows as a natural product of the tree, yet it is not equivalent to the tree; it is *kadosh*, and must be brought to the house of God. In the case of *terumot vemaasrot* (tithes), one must declare them to be special for the state of *kedusha* to obtain. In contrast, *bikkurim*, like the *bekhor*, are holy automatically, even though the seeds of *kedusha* are not found in the ground in which they grew.
9. "You shall not cook the kid in the milk of its mother" (34:26): *Ḥazal* explain the verse metaphorically – it is forbidden to cook or eat meat in milk. This is certainly a difficult mitzva to understand. One who is brought up in a halakhic framework naturally divides foods into two categories – dairy and meat – but there is no true logical basis for this division. After all, milk is an animal product; it goes together naturally with meat. Through its metaphor, the Torah declares the opposite – even though a kid is born of its mother and nurtured in her milk, we must set one against the other. This symbolizes the theme of this *berit* – things do not belong to their origin. In order to stress this to the utmost, the

21. The verse obligates "your males." This is, in fact, the only mitzva from which women are so explicitly exempt.

> most natural connection of all – that of a kid and its mother, his source and his nourishment – is to be broken.

As we noted, this *berit* is identical to the one found at the end of *Parashat Mishpatim,* before the sin of the golden calf. The point made here, that sanctity can arise in a mundane and unhallowed environment, is clearly the theme of Sinai as well, when God descended on the mountain to dwell among the Jewish People. In order for people to be the base of *kedusha,* the dwelling-place of God – "They shall make Me a tabernacle and I shall dwell in their midst" – the genetic fallacy must be overcome.

However, sin creates a major difference. It is one thing for mortal man to be the dwelling-place of God and the fountainhead of *kedusha* when he strives to serve God by accepting His Torah and obeying His laws. The sin of the golden calf logically destroys that dream – "*shiḥet amekha,*" "your people have corrupted." The same *berit* must be recreated, but in radically new circumstances. How can corruption be the basis of sanctity? The answer is found in the mystery of the Thirteen Attributes, the secret of "*nesiat ḥet*" – in "God before the sin, God after the sin."

History is completely different after sin because, amazingly, it continues.

About the Author

Rabbi Ezra Bick has been teaching at Yeshivat Har Etzion since he moved to Israel in 1977. He currently serves as Director of the Yeshiva's Israel Koschitzky Virtual Beit Midrash Project, which reaches tens of thousands of students worldwide. Rabbi Bick earned his *Semikha* from Yeshiva University and holds degrees in philosophy from Yeshiva University and Columbia University.

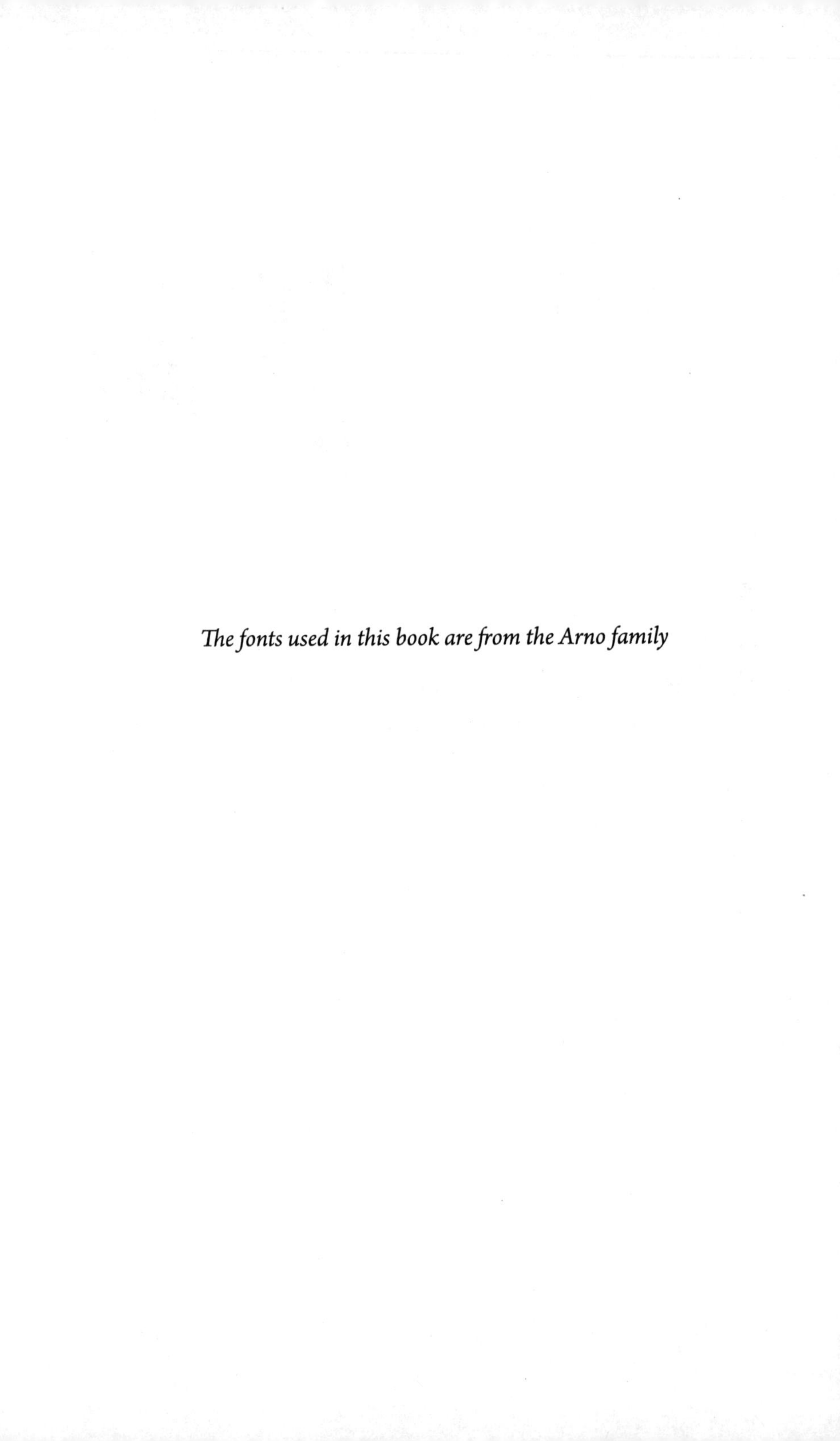

The fonts used in this book are from the Arno family

Maggid Books
The best of contemporary Jewish thought from
Koren Publishers Jerusalem